# GRAND CANYON
## V I S U A L

**JOHN F. HOFFMAN**

Mountain lion at Angel's Window, on the Grand Canyon's North Rim. DRAWING BY JOHN D. DAWSON

John Hance, first white settler at the Grand Canyon. PHOTO FROM U.S. DEPARTMENT OF THE INTERIOR, GRAND CANYON NATIONAL PARK, IDENTIFICATION NUMBER 825

Northern orioles nest in Havasu Canyon. DRAWING BY JOHN D. DAWSON

View across the Grand Canyon from Yavapai Point, on the South Rim. PHOTO BY FRANK L. MENDONCA

**WESTERN RECREATIONAL PUBLICATIONS**
P. O. BOX 6716
SAN DIEGO, CA 92166-0716



Manufactured in the United States of America

Library of Congress Catalog Number: 86-050723

International Standard Book Number: 0-934148-04-X

Printed by Rush Press San Diego, CA

**COVER PHOTOGRAPHS**

[**OUTSIDE FRONT COVER**] Grand Canyon in late afternoon, looking eastward from the South Rim near Yavapai Point. PHOTO BY DICK DIETRICH

[**INSIDE FRONT COVER**] Canyon vista to the west from Pima Point, on the South Rim. PHOTO BY FRANK L. MENDONCA

[**INSIDE BACK COVER**] View near lower end of the Grand Canyon's Marble Gorge. PHOTO BY TOM TILL

[**OUTSIDE BACK COVER**] Sunrise illuminates new snow on the South Rim's Mather Point. PHOTO BY TOM TILL

GRAND CANYON AND VICINITY
UTAH
Kanab
Fredonia
KAIBAB-PAIUTE INDIAN RESERVATION
389
NEVADA
ARIZONA
PARIAH RIVER
LAKE POWELL
Page
Lee's Ferry
89A
Jacob Lake
KAIBAB NATIONAL FOREST
67
98
Kayenta
163
160
NAVAJO INDIAN RESERVATION
HOPI INDIAN RESERVATION
89
GRAND
CANYON
NATIONAL
PARK
Toroweap Overlook
Hualapai Hilltop
HAVASUPAI INDIAN RESERVATION
LAKE MEAD
Pearce Ferry
HUALAPAI INDIAN RESERVATION
COLORADO RIVER
Diamond Creek
Grand Canyon Village
64
180
KAIBAB NATIONAL FOREST
LITTLE COLORADO RIVER
Tuba City
264
NAVAJO INDIAN RES.
KAIBAB
NATIONAL
FOREST
Park Entrance Station
Saddle Mountain
Boundary
Ridge
NAVAJO INDIAN RESERVATION
NORTH
RIM
Point Imperial
Kolb Natural Bridge
Mount Hayden
NANKOWEAP CANYON
NANKOWEAP MESA
MARBLE
GORGE
Vista Encantadora
Painted Desert Viewpoint
Duppa Butte
Kwagunt Butte
Uncle Jim Point
WALHALLA
PLATEAU
Atoko Point
Siegfried Pyre
Chuar Butte
LITTLE COLORADO RIVER
Cape Solitude
Point Sublime
THE DRAGON
Dragon Head
Grand Canyon Lodge
Bright Angel Point
HINDU
AMPHITHEATER
Tiyo Point
Widforss Point
Shiva Temple
Osiris Temple
Tower of Ra
Isis Temple
Buddha Temple
Deva Temple
Brahma Temple
Thor Temple
Juno Temple
Temple Butte
Cape Final
Jupiter Temple
Venus Temple
Tower of Set
Cheops Pyramid
Zoroaster Temple
OTTOMAN
AMPHITHEATER
Angel's Window
Apollo Temple
Phantom Ranch
NORTH
BRIGHT ANGEL CANYON
Cape Royal
Vishnu Temple
Angel's Gate
Wotan's Throne
Suspension Bridge
UPPER
Plateau Point
BRIGHT ANGEL TRAIL
Indian Gardens
SOUTH KAIBAB TRAIL
GRANITE
COLORADO
RIVER
GORGE
PAINTED
DESERT
Hermit's Rest
Grand Canyon Village
SOUTH
Park Entrance Station
Horseshoe Mesa
RED CANYON
Desert View
Park Entrance Station
Lipan Point
Tusayan Ruins
Grandview Point
Moran Point
Sinking Ship
180
64
KAIBAB
RIM
NATIONAL
FOREST

# GEOGRAPHY

Many large buttes rise from the depths of the Grand Canyon. Such single, isolated eminences elsewhere would be called mountains.
PHOTO BY TOM TILL

THE GRAND CANYON IS OFTEN acclaimed the most awe inspiring and spectacular natural feature on earth. Listed as one of the Seven Natural Wonders of the World, the Canyon in 1919 became a United States national park, and in 1979 was named a World Heritage Site, a place which has such superlative natural and cultural features that it is considered to have universal value for all humankind.

Carved by the Colorado River, the Grand Canyon slices deep into the Colorado Plateau, a vast upland of colorful and rugged terrain that forms one of the most strikingly scenic landscapes of the American West—and the World. The Canyon trends in a generally east-to-west direction across nearly 278 miles of northern Arizona. Ranging in width from less than a mile to more than 18 miles, the Canyon is more than a mile deep in places. Grand Canyon National Park encompasses much of the chasm, covering nearly 1,900 square miles.

Along both rims, the topography is relatively level. In contrast, relief within the Grand Canyon is characterized by steep slopes and massive, precipitous cliffs. Canyon altitudes range from about 1,200 feet above sea level in the chasm's extreme western end on Lake Mead, to 8,803 feet at Point Imperial on the edge of the North Rim. Away from the North Rim, in places the surface rises even higher, and at one spot near the Park's northern boundary attains 9,165 feet. Elevations on the South Rim vary from 6,000 to 7,500 feet, or 1,000 to 2,000 feet lower than on the North Rim. On the Canyon's bottom, Phantom Ranch, at an elevation of 2,570 feet, lies about 4,400 feet below Grand Canyon Village on the South Rim, and nearly 5,600 feet lower than Grand Canyon Lodge on the North Rim.

**Grand Canyon Climatological Summary**

| | NORTH RIM | SOUTH RIM | PHANTOM RANCH |
|---|---|---|---|
| Temperature, °F. | | | |
| January average | 28.7 | 30.5 | 46.3 |
| July average | 61.7 | 69.4 | 91.9 |
| Annual average | 44.0 | 48.8 | 69.2 |
| Precipitation, inches | | | |
| Rainfall, average | 22.78 | 14.46 | 8.39 |
| Snowfall, average | 128.70 | 64.90 | 0.20 |

Because of its great length and depth, the Grand Canyon includes many different physical and biological environments. Climates range from desert to subarctic, or the same climatic variation that exists from northern Mexico to central Canada.

## VAN LOON'S BOX

More than fifty years ago, noted author and illustrator Hendrik Willem Van Loon, a Dutch-born immigrant to the United States, offered a fascinating perspective on the size of the Grand Canyon—and on the insignificance of the human race. Van Loon calculated that all of the people then alive could be packed into an enormous box measuring half-a-mile square. If pushed over the edge of the Grand Canyon, the box would crash to the deep chasm's bottom, where it would eventually crumble. All that would mark where humanity lay buried would be a mound. "The astronomers on distant and nearby planets," Van Loon said, "would have noticed nothing out of the ordinary." The Earth would continue to orbit the Sun and the forces of erosion would continue to work relentlessly on the Grand Canyon. "And," declared Van Loon, "that would be all."

SKETCH FROM *VAN LOON'S GEOGRAPHY* © 1932 BY HENDRIK WILLEM VAN LOON. REPRINTED BY PERMISSION OF SIMON AND SCHUSTER, INC.

**[PAGES 2-3]** A rainbow fashions a kaleidoscopic arc in the Grand Canyon.
PHOTO BY TOM TILL

The Grand Canyon has a variety of natural environments, ranging from desert deep on the chasm's bottom to subarctic on its high North Rim. Altitude is of major importance to the Canyon, shaping its climates and its vegetation.

## LOCATION

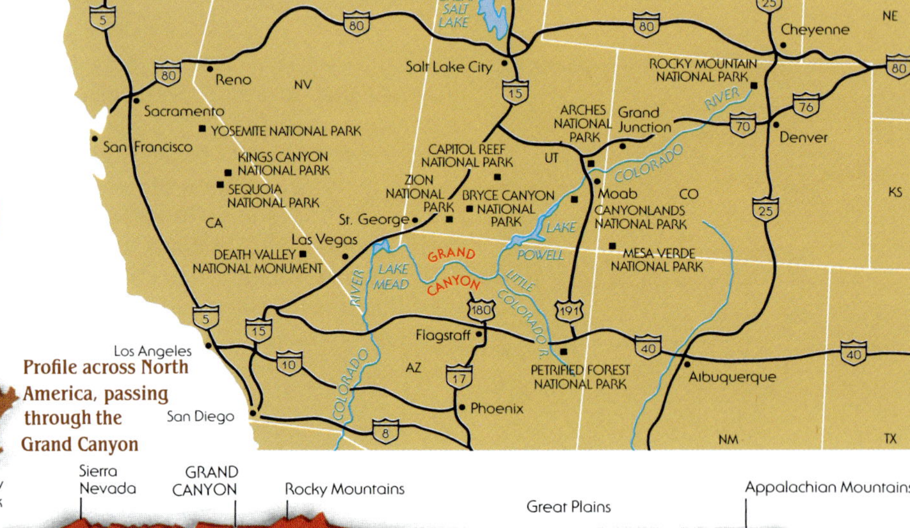


Profile across North America, passing through the Grand Canyon

Seven plateaus border the Grand Canyon. All are subdivisions of the Colorado Plateau's southwestern area.

**Air-line mileages from the Grand Canyon**

| UNITED STATES | | WORLD | |
|---|---|---|---|
| Anchorage, AK | 2,456 | Athens, Greece | 6,645 |
| Atlanta, GA | 1,555 | Auckland, New Zealand | 6,848 |
| Baltimore, MD | 1,940 | Bangkok, Thailand | 8,463 |
| Boston, MA | 2,225 | Beirut, Lebanon | 7,228 |
| Chicago, IL | 1,376 | Bombay, India | 8,694 |
| Cleveland, OH | 1,675 | Buenos Aires, Argentina | 5,904 |
| Dallas, TX | 867 | Cairo, Egypt | 7,338 |
| Denver, CO | 482 | Copenhagen, Denmark | 5,368 |
| Detroit, MI | 1,612 | London, United Kingdom | 5,172 |
| Honolulu, HI | 2,964 | Madrid, Spain | 5,509 |
| Houston, TX | 1,021 | Manila, Philippines | 7,580 |
| Los Angeles, CA | 384 | Mexico City, Mexico | 1,329 |
| Milwaukee, WI | 1,380 | Montreal, Canada | 2,108 |
| New Orleans, LA | 1,307 | Moscow, U.S.S.R | 5,912 |
| New York, NY | 2,075 | Ottawa, Canada | 2,006 |
| Philadelphia, PA | 2,015 | Paris, France | 5,372 |
| Phoenix, AZ | 172 | Peking, China | 6,427 |
| Portland, OR | 917 | Rio de Janeiro, Brazil | 6,002 |
| St. Louis, MO | 1,209 | Rome, Italy | 6,060 |
| Salt Lake City, UT | 384 | Stockholm, Sweden | 5,315 |
| San Diego, CA | 359 | Sydney, Australia | 7,867 |
| San Francisco, CA | 625 | Tokyo, Japan | 5,736 |
| Seattle, WA | 1,018 | Toronto, Canada | 1,809 |
| Washington, D.C. | 1,919 | Vancouver, Canada | 1,312 |

## CANYON DIMENSIONS

| | |
|---|---|
| Length | 277.7 miles |
| Width | Less than 1 mile to more than 18 miles |
| Depth | Maximum, about 6,000 feet |

Longitudinal profile of the Colorado River through the Grand Canyon

# CLIMATE

The Grand Canyon's great range of altitudes—from 1,200 to 9,100 feet—results in a wide variety of climates, from desert to subarctic.

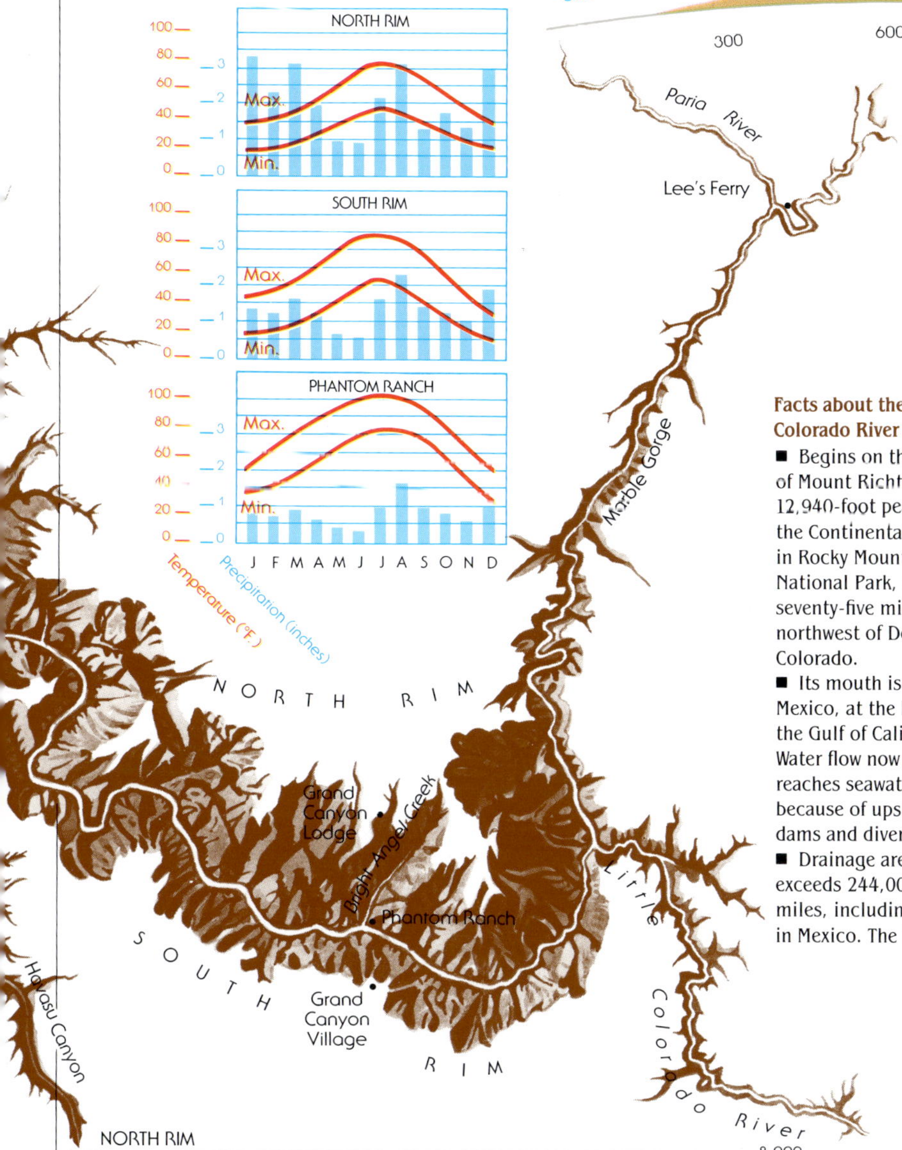

Long profile of the Colorado River (vertical exaggeration 250 times)

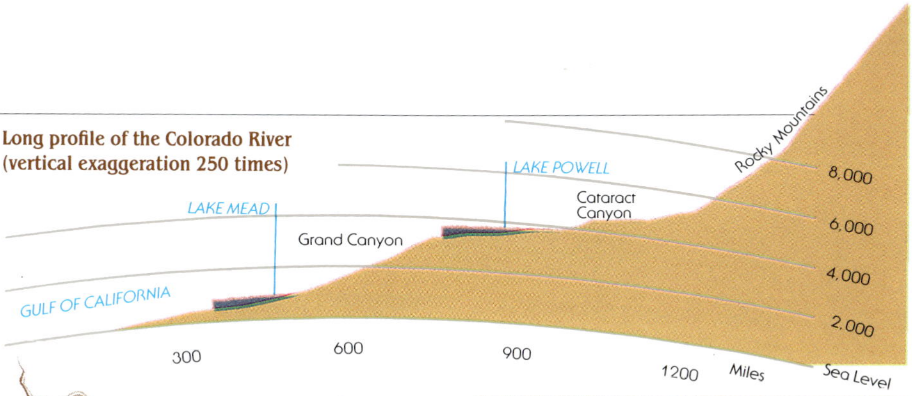

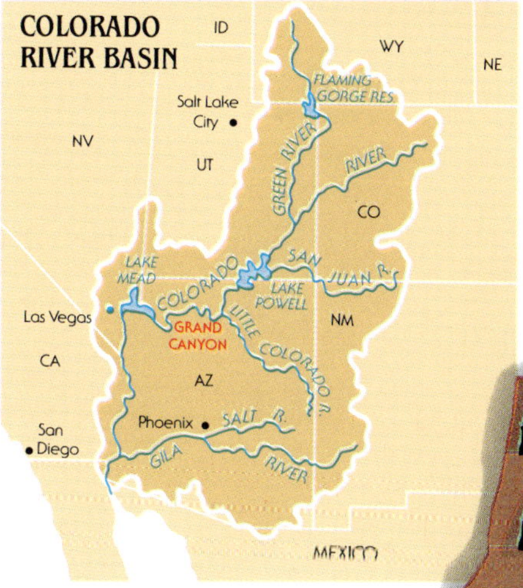

**Facts about the Colorado River**

- Begins on the slopes of Mount Richthofen, a 12,940-foot peak on the Continental Divide in Rocky Mountain National Park, about seventy-five miles northwest of Denver, Colorado.
- Its mouth is in Mexico, at the head of the Gulf of California. Water flow now seldom reaches seawater because of upstream dams and diversions.
- Drainage area exceeds 244,000 square miles, including 1,000 in Mexico. The basin spreads over more than one-twelfth of the contiguous United States.
- Its length is more than 1,450 miles, with the last 90 miles lying in Mexico.
- From its headwaters to its mouth, the Colorado's descent is nearly two-and-a-half miles.

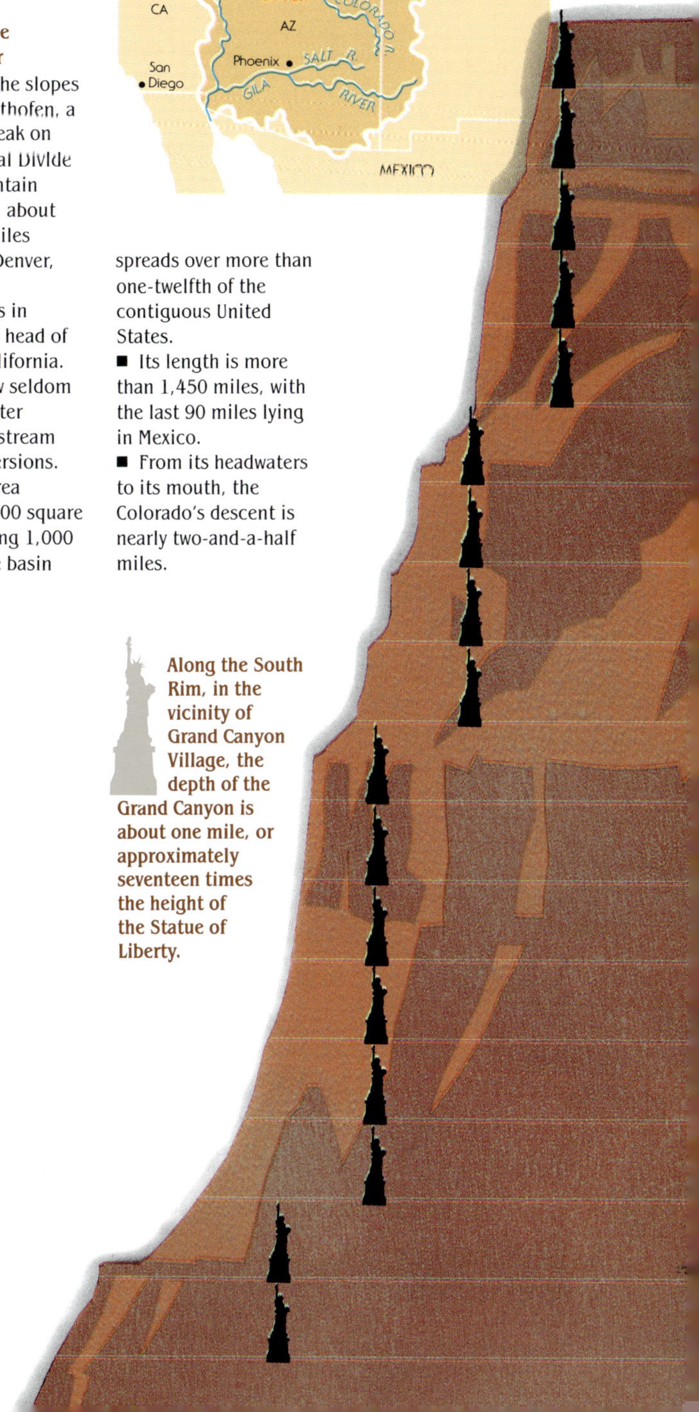

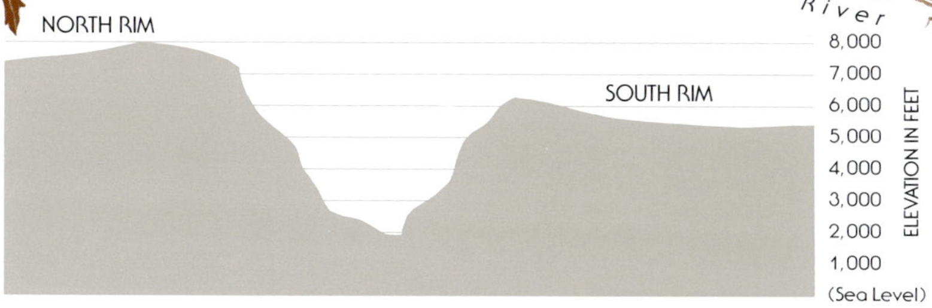

Grand Canyon's North Rim is 1,000 to 2,000 feet higher than its South Rim

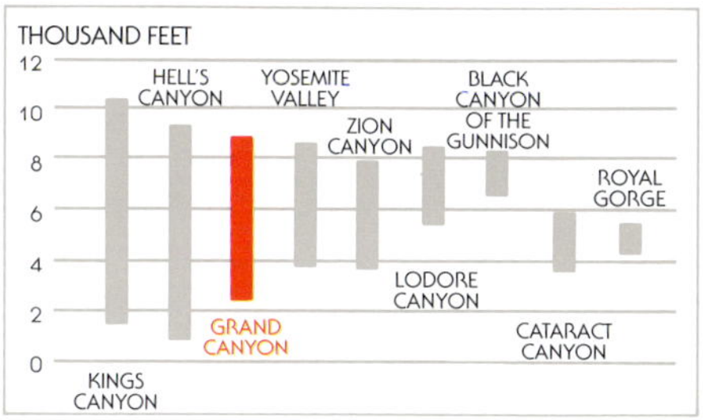

Comparative depths of major canyons in the United States

Along the South Rim, in the vicinity of Grand Canyon Village, the depth of the Grand Canyon is about one mile, or approximately seventeen times the height of the Statue of Liberty.

# GEOLOGY

Bighorn sheep standing on remnant of a basalt lava flow in the western Grand Canyon.
PHOTO BY TOM TILL

THE GRAND CANYON PRESENTS an unrivaled view into the Earth's geologic history. From the Canyon's Paleozoic-era rims to the bottom of its Precambrian-age inner gorge, nearly 2 billion years of time are represented in the exposed rocks, or about two-fifths of the Earth's estimated age of 5 billion years. Certainly its geologic significance and its scenic magnificence justify calling the Grand Canyon the world's most impressive chasm.

The great Canyon cuts deeply into the southwestern part of the Colorado Plateau, in northern Arizona. Renowned for its spectacular and colorful topography, the vast, high plateau covers about 130,000 square miles, lying in the American West between the Southern Rocky Mountains and the Basin and Range. The plateau straddles Four Corners, the only point in the country where four state boundaries meet, those of Colorado, New Mexico, Arizona, and Utah.

One of thirty-four natural regions composing the United States, the Colorado Plateau has distinctive features which give it a unique character. All of these features are found also at the Grand Canyon. The plateau is primarily differentiated from the other regions by:

- Extensive areas of relatively horizontal strata of sedimentary rocks, deposited in layer-cake fashion.
- High altitudes, generally more than a mile above sea level.
- Deeply entrenched watercourses, creating steep-walled canyons and gorges.
- Pronounced, angular topography, accentuated by bold and precipitous escarpments and massive cliffs.
- Conspicuous and expansive tracts of nearly barren or naked rock, appropriately called *slickrock*.
- A wide, often brilliant, range of rock and soil colors.
- Igneous features, including volcanoes, cinder cones, and lava flows.
- Generally semiarid climatic conditions.
- Predominantly sparse vegetative cover.

Uplift of the Colorado Plateau by massive forces within the Earth set the stage for the Colorado River to cut downward, entrenching its channel. The River, however, cuts only a vertical channel, whereas the width of the Grand Canyon—in places more than eighteen miles across—results from physical and chemical processes of weathering and erosion of the chasm's walls and along the Colorado's tributaries and side canyons.

## TRAVERTINE FALLS

Some of the most spectacular travertine deposits in the world are found in the western Grand Canyon. Travertine Falls, on the south bank of the Colorado at Mile 230.5, is particularly striking. Travertine, a creamy-colored, porous limestone, is usually formed by the evaporation of spring water. The rock's principal constituent is calcite, a mineral composed of calcium carbonate. Extensive spring deposits on the walls of Travertine Canyon, which joins the Colorado on the south at Mile 229, have given that gorge its name. In the western Grand Canyon, the Colorado's tributaries are so rich in calcium carbonate that they deposit travertine, and along Havasu Creek these deposits have formed low dams. Also, spray from the creek's waterfalls deposits travertine on nearby canyon walls.
PHOTO BY TOM TILL

[OPPOSITE PAGE] Pompey's Pillar, near Grandview Point on the South Rim, is an outlier of the Kaibab Limestone formation, the uppermost layer of the Grand Canyon. Erosional forces separated the column from the main formation. The pillar's bizarre shape resulted from different rates of erosion of its horizontal strata which have varying hardnesses. Geologists call such irregularly shaped pillars *hoodoos*. The large, rectangular "balanced rock" atop this pillar is not sitting loose in a precarious position, but is physically part of the column. About 1900, George Wharton James, author of two books on the Grand Canyon, named the pillar for Pompey (106-48 B.C.), Roman statesman and general, who was a rival of Caesar.
PHOTO BY TOM TILL

[PAGES 8-9] Lightning flashes, seen from Point Imperial on North Rim.
PHOTO BY TOM BEAN

Only about 4 million years were required for the Grand Canyon to be eroded to its awesome dimensions. But the many geological events leading eventually to the present Canyon began at its future site long before that—at least 2 billion years ago.

**2 billion years ago:** Sediments and volcanic material accumulated.

**1.7 billion years ago:** Mountains are uplifted; rocks metamorphosed into Vishnu Schist.

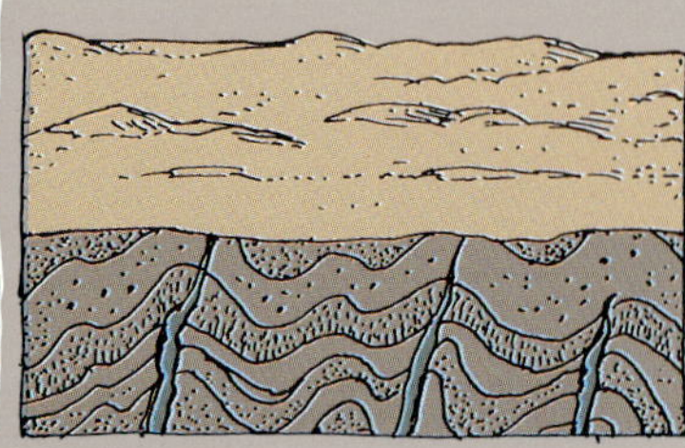

**1.5 billion years ago:** Mountains eroded to a nearly level plain.

**1.2 billion years ago:** Plain subsided; Grand Canyon Supergroup layers deposited.

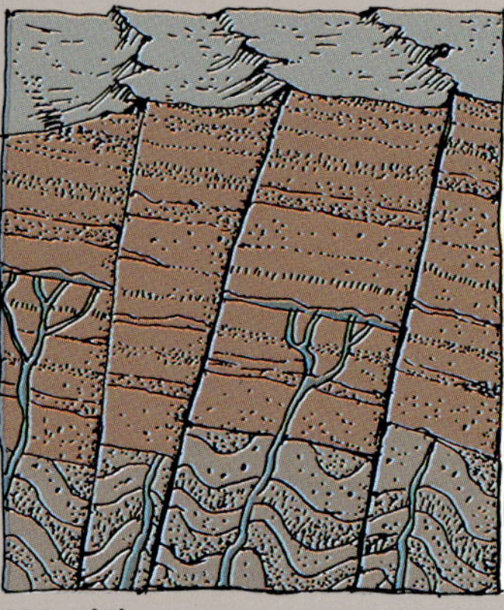

**800 million years ago:** Fault-block mountains formed.

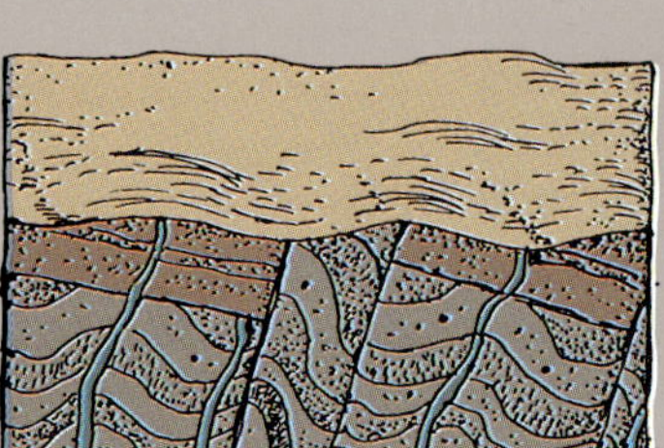

**700 million years ago:** Mountains eroded to hilly topography.

**600 million years ago:** Area subsided; Paleozoic layers deposited.

**230 million years ago:** Mesozoic sediments deposited.

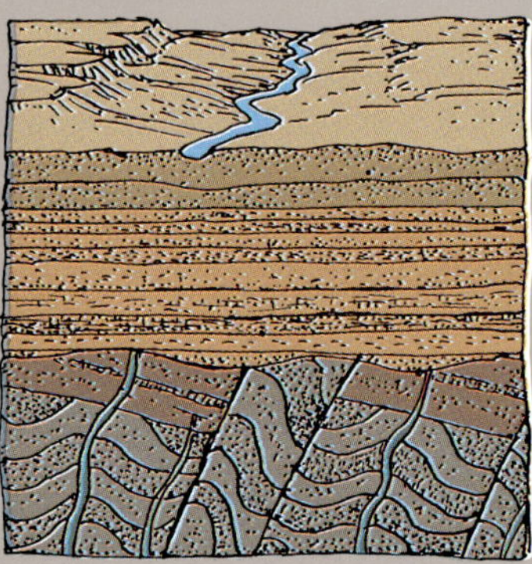

**65 million years ago:** Uplift and erosion of Mesozoic sediments.

**4 million years:** Colorado River began to cut the Grand Canyon; volcanic activity within the last 1 million years in the western Canyon.

Ten major, large-scale geological events occurred during the last 2 billion years in what is today's Grand Canyon region. When each event began and ended can be only approximated. However, evidence that they happened can be seen in rocks exposed in the Canyon's walls. Obviously, cutting of the chasm did not end topographical change in the region. Geological processes continue there unabated, and the future—measured in millions of years—will bring many different landscapes to the area now dominated by the Grand Canyon.

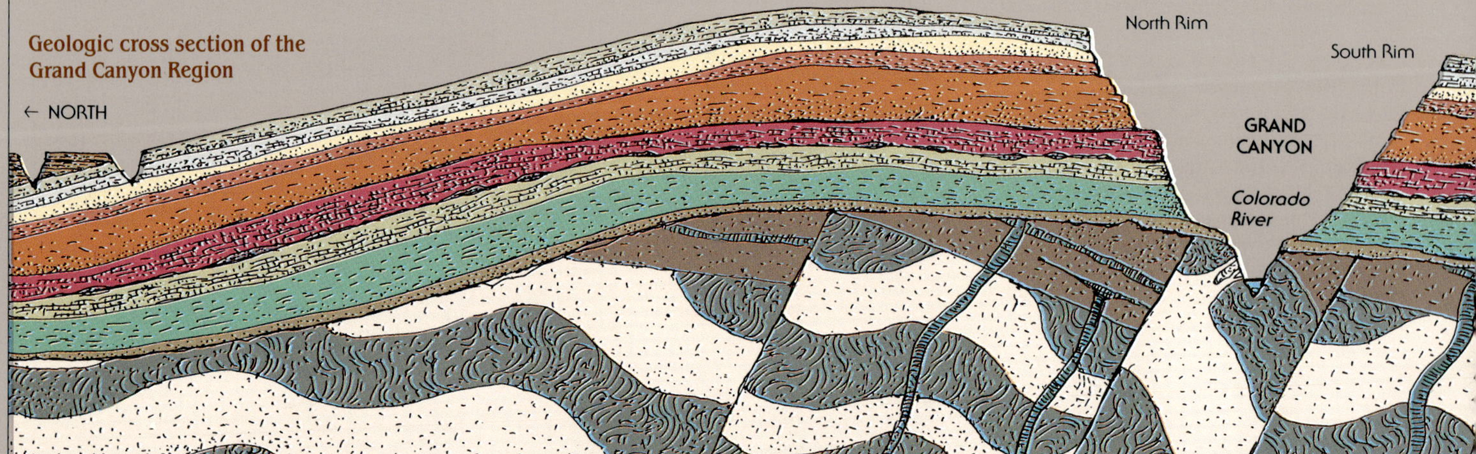


Geologic cross section of the Grand Canyon Region

| THICKNESS (feet) | DEPOSITIONAL ENVIRONMENT | AGE (millions of years ago) | GEOLOGIC TIME: Era | GEOLOGIC TIME: Period |
|---|---|---|---|---|
| 300-500 | sea | 250 | PALEOZOIC | Middle Permian |
| 250-450 | sea | 260 | | |
| 50-350 | desert | 270 | | |
| 250-1,000 | floodplain | 280 | | Early Permian |
| 950-1,350 | swamp | 300 | | Pennsyl-vanian |
| 450-700 | sea | 330 | | Early and Middle Mississip-pian |
| 30-1,000 | sea | 370 | | Late Devonian |
| DISCONFORMITY | | 400-500 | | Silurian and Ordovician |
| 50-1,000 | sea | 530 | | Middle Cambrian |
| 200-450 | sea | 540 | | Early and Middle Cambrian |
| 100-300 | sea | 550 | | Early Cambrian |
| THE GREAT UNCONFORMITY | | 570-800 | | |
| 15,000 | sea | 800-1,200 | PRECAMBRIAN | Late |
| | metamor-phosed sea sediments | 1,700 | | Early |
| | molten intrusion | | | |

Sequence of rock formations exposed in the Grand Canyon

Several times in the last 1 million years, volcanic activity has occurred in the western Grand Canyon. Displays of this volcanism give certain areas of the western Canyon a topographical appearance strikingly different than the landscape in the eastern Canyon. In terms of geologic time, the western Canyon's volcanic activity is recent. Evidence of this igneous action includes cinder cones, lava flows, and dikes, and extends for more than 80 miles down the Canyon, starting near Colorado River Mile 178.

[TOP] Lava flows have poured into the Canyon at least ten times in the last 1 million years. Lava has come from Prospect Canyon, Toroweap Valley, and Whitmore Wash. These flows have blocked the Colorado River, creating dams which formed temporary lakes. The largest dam was about 1,400 feet high, and probably backed a lake 150 miles up canyon. The artist's illustration shows how a dam may have looked where Lava Falls, largest rapid in the Canyon, is now at River Mile 179.3.
DRAWING BY JOHN D. DAWSON.

[LEFT] Vulcan's Throne, a prominent landmark of western Grand Canyon, is a large cinder cone perched on the rim of the Esplanade, near Toroweap Overlook. This cone, about a mile in diameter, rises 567 feet above the benchland, and towers some 3,500 feet above the Colorado River at Lava Falls.
PHOTO BY TOM TILL

A basalt lava flow in the western Grand Canyon has *columnar jointing,* formed by shrinkage of the thick lava as it slowly cooled, creating long prisms with a distinctive hexagonal pattern.
PHOTO BY TOM TILL

Final excavation of the Grand Canyon began after the opening of the Gulf of California. When the gulf began to form, about 5 million years ago, the ancestral Colorado ran into ancient Lake Bidahochi, from which flowed the ancestral Río Grande. As the gulf opened, the ancient Hualapai River eroded headward from the gulf and captured the ancestral Colorado, creating the modern River which cut the Grand Canyon to its present depth.

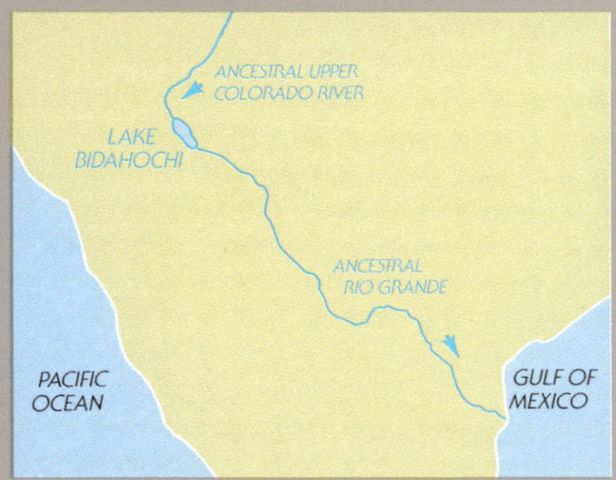

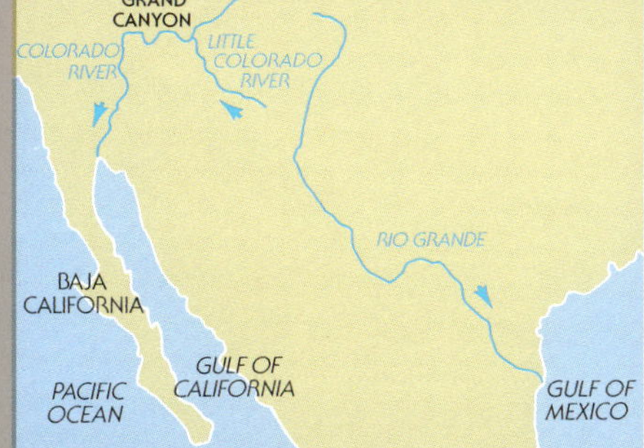


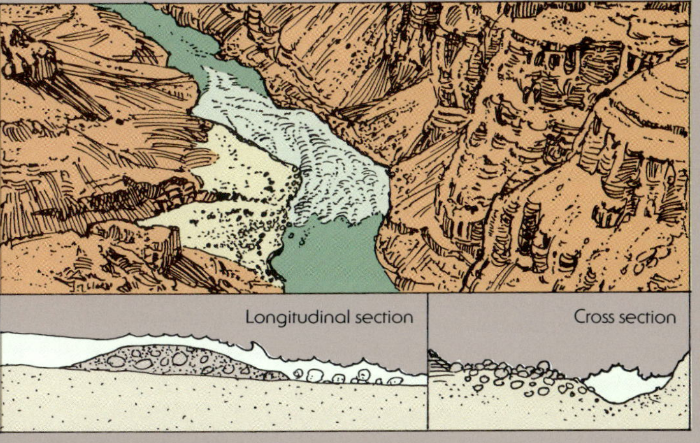


Most of the Colorado's rapids in the Grand Canyon form at the mouths of tributaries, where debris is washed into the River, creating rocky dams. As the River rushes over these dams, rapids are formed. The presence, configuration, and severity of rapids depend upon the River's volume. At low stages, rapids are generally more severe.
DRAWING BY JOHN D. DAWSON

Profiles of the Grand Canyon show how the topography and the width of the chasm are controlled by the types of rocks through which the Colorado River has cut. Hard formations—granites, schists, limestones, and sandstones—erode into cliffs and steep slopes, while softer rocks—shales and siltstones—form slopes.
PAPER SCULPTURE BY JOHN ODAM

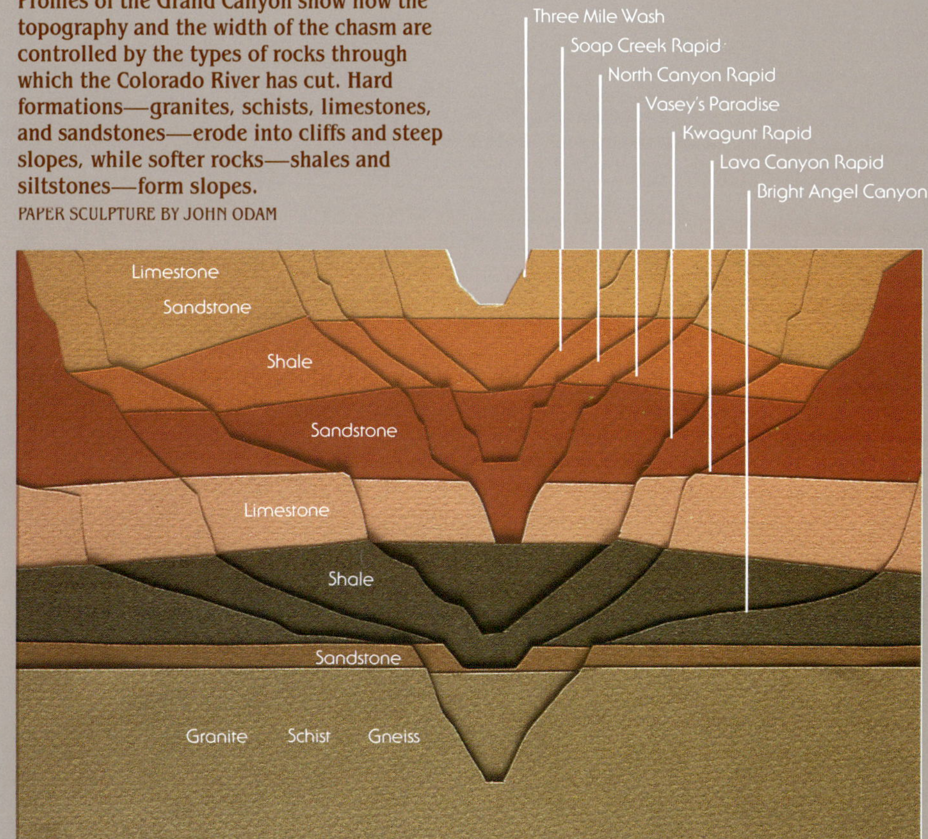


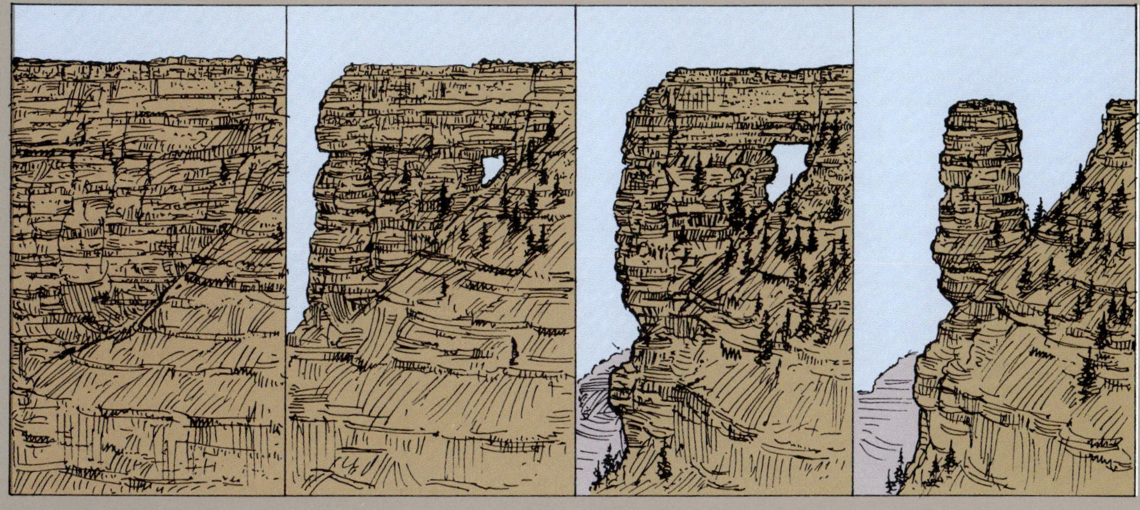

Angel's Window, near Cape Royal, on the North Rim, is one of the Grand Canyon's distinctive features. The natural arch formed by erosional processes in a narrow projection of Kaibab Limestone. All landforms, though inanimate, have "life cycles." Angel's Window has attained "maturity," and eventually its span will collapse, marking its "death."
DRAWING BY JOHN D. DAWSON

# WILDLIFE

THE GRAND CANYON OFFERS an astonishing diversity of plant and animal life. Among the flora, more than a thousand different flowering plants have been recorded. Fauna documented include at least 299 species of birds, 74 kinds of mammals, 8 species of amphibians, and 40 kinds of reptiles.

The Canyon's rich variety of plant and animal life can be credited largely to a single physical factor: altitude. The lowest elevation, found at the chasm's extreme western end, is about 1,200 feet; the highest—9,100 feet—is on the North Rim. Within this 7,900-foot vertical span are many different environments, ranging from torrid desert on the Canyon floor to subalpine forests atop the North Rim. These various environments replicate, in miniature, the range of plant and animal habitats encountered from northern Mexico to Alaska.

The vertical climatic bands create distinct *life zones.* Seven of these zones have been recognized on the North American continent, of which four have been identified at the Grand Canyon. From lowest to highest altitude, the Canyon zones are: Lower Sonoran, Upper Sonoran, Transition, and Canadian.

The Lower Sonoran Zone is equivalent to desert, with annual precipitation a mere three to eleven inches. This zone is found in the western Grand Canyon, generally below 2,000 feet altitude.

The Upper Sonoran Zone includes desert scrub and piñon-juniper woodland, with elevations ranging from 2,000 to 7,000 feet. Precipitation varies from about seven to twenty-two inches. The benchlands and rims of the Canyon are included in the Upper Sonoran.

The Transition Zone is equivalent to the yellow-pine—or ponderosa—forest. Yearly precipitation within this zone is approximately eighteen to twenty-six inches. Elevation of the forest ordinarily lies between 6,500 and 7,400 feet. Prominent stands of this forest are found on both rims of the Canyon.

The Canadian Zone is exemplified by the spruce-fir forest and the mountain grassland. This zone's elevation is from about 8,000 feet to 8,800 feet, where precipitation is approximately twenty-five to thirty inches annually. The Canadian occurs only on the Canyon's North Rim.

Within life zones are *biotic communities*, or groups of plants and animals inhabiting and interacting in a common area.

## KAIBAB SQUIRREL

Inhabiting the yellow-pine woodland of the North Rim, the Kaibab squirrel is the only mammal unique to the Grand Canyon; its entire range lies strictly on the North Rim, extending only a short distance beyond the Park's northern boundary. This large, tree-dwelling squirrel has a distinctive white tail. Its body color is grayish, and its ears have tufts or tassels. Overall length for this mammal is about twenty inches, with the tail accounting for slightly less than half of the length. Nests are built high in ponderosa, or yellow, pines. Kaibab squirrels feed primarily on ponderosa-pine seeds and inner bark, and in summertime they may also eat mushrooms. This mammal—today scarce—is now listed as a rare and endangered wildlife species. The Kaibab closely resembles the Abert squirrel, which lives at the Grand Canyon only on the South Rim, but also occurs in some other areas of the Southwest. Like the Kaibab, the Aberts are tassel-eared, and are of the same size and color, except that the Abert's tail is gray on top with a white underside while the Kaibab's tail is all white.

PHOTO © BY TOM & PAT LEESON

[OPPOSITE PAGE] Three mule deer at the Canyon's edge, along the Rim Trail on the South Rim.
PHOTO BY TOM BEAN

[PAGES 16-17] Sunrise in mid-August, viewed from near Mather Point on South Rim, heralds a new day at the Grand Canyon.
PHOTO BY GARY LADD

Biologists divide the plants and animals of the Grand Canyon into six major groups called *biotic communities.* Usually these communities are named for the dominant plant species which give each group its special character. Flora and fauna that define one community may also be found in other groups but are not dominant there. These assemblages are influenced by several physical factors including climate, rock and soil types, and altitude.The six principal communities at the Canyon are: piñon-juniper woodland, desert scrub, yellow-pine woodland, spruce-fir forest, mountain grassland, and streamside.

1 Kaibab squirrel
2 Mule deer
3 Bobcat
4 Porcupine
5 Deer mouse
6 Common flicker
7 Steller's jay
8 Wild turkey
9 Western bluebird
10 Great Basin gopher snake
11 Northern plateau lizard

A Ponderosa (yellow) pine
B Gambel oak
C Mountain mahogany
D Blue elderberry

**Yellow-Pine Woodland Community**

The yellow-pined woodland is more extensive on the Grand Canyon's North Rim than on the South Rim. On the North Rim, the community lies between 7,200 and 8,200 feet altitude, while on the South Rim the woodland is found between 7,000 and 7,400 feet. Rainfall is normally in excess of twenty inches annually. The forest is open, with grasses and shrubs usually present on the floor.

DRAWING BY JOHN D. DAWSON

**Piñon-Juniper Woodland Community**

The piñon-juniper woodland occurs along the rims of the Grand Canyon and on the summits of some of the buttes rising in the canyon. This community forms a belt between the desert scrub and the yellow-pine woodland. Annual precipitation in the piñon-juniper woodland is between ten and twenty inches. The community's name is derived from its two dominant plant species: the Utah juniper and the piñon pine. These short evergreens form open woodlands, usually with trees far enough apart that their branches do not touch. Interspersed with the small trees are shrubs and patches of bare ground or rock. The diminutive stature of the junipers and piñons has resulted in this woodland being aptly called the "Pygmy Forest." The pine's name is often spelled "pinyon," the Anglicized equivalent of the Spanish noun "piñon."

DRAWING BY JOHN D. DAWSON

1 Mountain lion
2 Mule deer
3 Gray fox
4 Desert cottontail
5 Cliff chipmunk
6 Common raven
7 Hairy woodpecker

8 Piñon jay
9 Yellow-backed spiny lizard
10 Southern plateau lizard
11 Mountain short-horned lizard
12 Sonoran gopher snake

A Piñon pine
B Utah juniper
C Gambel oak
D Cliff rose
E Mormon tea
F Rabbitbrush
G Banana yucca

**Spruce-Fir Forest and Mountain Grassland Communities**

Restricted to elevations generally above 8,200 feet on the Grand Canyon's North Rim is a spruce-fir forest with a mixing of aspens. This community experiences cold winters with heavy snowfall, and has a short growing season of about three months. The forest's canopy is dense, with few shrubs and grasses. Mosses and lichens prevail. In shallow valleys, scattered through the spruce-fir forest, are meadows termed by biologists the mountain grasslands community.

DRAWING BY JOHN D. DAWSON

1 Mule deer
2 Bobcat
3 Porcupine
4 Red squirrel
5 Deer mouse
6 Uinta chipmunk
7 Golden-mantled ground squirrel
8 Northern pocket gopher
9 Mountain bluebird
10 Gray-headed junco
11 Cassin's finch

A White fir
B Blue spruce
C Aspen
D Engelmann spruce
E Douglas fir
F Yarrow
G Letterman needlegrass
H Kentucky bluegrass

### Desert Scrub Community

Desert scrub is found on the benchlands (Tonto Plateau and the Esplanade), and in the inner gorges away from the Colorado River. The community exists primarily below 4,500 feet altitude. Its predominant plant is the blackbrush. The community is characterized by generally low, widely spaced, woody stemmed, and small-leaved bushes which are drought resistant. Certain of the plants are also salt tolerant.

DRAWING BY JOHN D. DAWSON

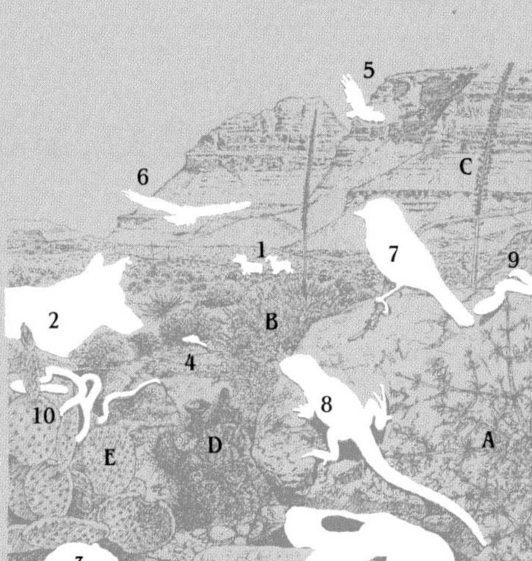


1 Bighorn
2 Coyote
3 Ord's kangaroo rat
4 Desert wood rat
5 Turkey vulture
6 Red-tailed hawk
7 Black-throated sparrow
8 Collared lizard
9 California kingsnake
10 Desert striped whipsnake
11 Grand Canyon rattlesnake

A Blackbrush
B Four-wing saltbush
C Utah agave
D Claretcup hedgehog
E Beavertail

### Streamside Community

The streamside or *riparian* community occurs on constantly moist soil along the margins of perennial and intermittent streams. Where these plants are thickly massed, they stand out in striking contrast to the generally sparse, low, and scrubby plants that grow on less moist ground. The greatest concentration and variety of animal life found at the Grand Canyon occur within the streamside community.

DRAWING BY JOHN D. DAWSON

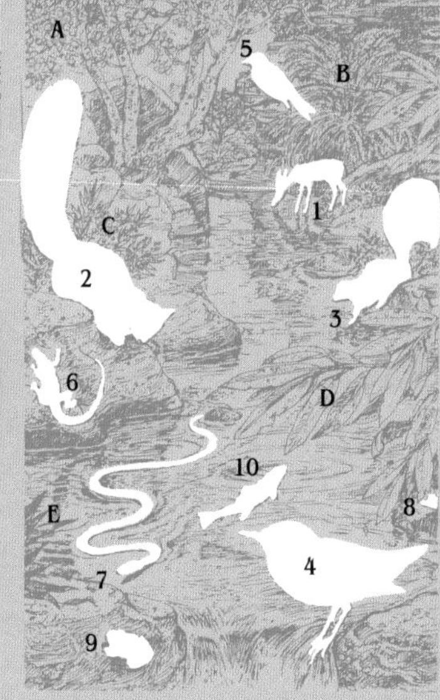


1 Mule deer
2 Ringtail
3 Spotted skunk
4 American dipper
5 Lesser goldfinch
6 Northern whiptail
7 Desert striped whipsnake
8 Rocky Mountain toad
9 Canyon tree frog
10 Rainbow trout

A Cottonwood
B Tamarisk
C Seep-willow
D Willow
E Arrowweed

[PAGES 24–25] From Yaki Point on the South Rim, a winter sunrise reveals an ocean of clouds flooding the Canyon, with flat-topped Wotan's Throne and pyramid-shaped Vishnu Temple projecting like islands off the point of North Rim's Cape Royal.

PHOTO BY GARY LADD

# INDIANS

PALEO-INDIANS, THE GRAND CANYON'S first inhabitants, arrived there about 11,000 years ago. These ancient Indians were descendants of Asian people who began to migrate to North America at least 25,000 years earlier, during the Ice Age.

Slowly the Paleo-Indian way of life changed, and by some 7,500 years ago a new culture—the Archaic—had developed. Like their Paleo-Indian ancestors the Archaic people were hunters, but unlike the Paleo-Indians, the Archaics hunted modern species which were smaller than the Ice Age animals.

The earliest human artifacts discovered at the Grand Canyon are from the Archaic period. These are split-twig animal figurines which have been determined by radioactive dating to be about 4,000 years old. Although their purpose is unknown, the animal replicas may have been fetishes used in hunting ceremonies.

The Archaic period ended at the Canyon about 3,000 years ago. For the next millennium and a half there is no evidence that people lived there. Then, some 1,500 years ago, the Anasazi entered the eastern Grand Canyon and the Cohonina migrated into its western section.

More than 2,000 Anasazi sites have been found at the Canyon. Anasazi raised corn, beans, and squash, and they also hunted and gathered foodstuffs. They made pottery and baskets, and carved and painted images on rocks. Approximately 800 years ago the Anasazi abandoned the Canyon, moving eastward to become the ancestors of today's Hopi Indians.

The Anasazi traded with their friendly western neighbors, the Cohonina. Like the Anasazi, the Cohonina also practiced agriculture. They abandoned the Canyon when the Anasazi did, possibly joining their eastward exodus.

About 150 years later, the Cerbat Indians moved into the western Grand Canyon. Their descendants are the Hualapai and Havasupai Indians who today live on separate reservations in the western Canyon, south of the Colorado River.

Approximately the same time the Cerbats arrived, the Southern Paiute Indians began making hunting and gathering trips to the Canyon's North Rim. Southern Paiutes still live north of the Canyon.

Last of the Indian groups to arrive at the Grand Canyon, about 600 years ago, were the Navajos. Their origins have been traced to Canada. The Navajo Reservation borders the eastern side of the Canyon.

## ROCK ART

Indian rock art is found at many sites in the Grand Canyon. Indian artists carved or painted a variety of forms, including geometric designs, symbolized animals, and humanoid figures. While the purpose of their art is not known, some of it may have had religious significance, or been associated with hunting. Archeologists called Indian carvings *petroglyphs*, and their paintings *pictographs*. Indian artists usually made petroglyphs by pecking or scratching their designs on large rocks or cliff faces with hammerstones or choppers. Desert-varnished rock surfaces were well-suited for petroglyphs since the natural, darker patina, when cut through, exposed the underlying, lighter-colored rock. Pictographs were made by coating stone surfaces with paints made from rock and plant materials. Those at Two-Mile Corner on the Bright Angel Trail were probably painted by the Havasupai.
PHOTO BY TOM BEAN

**[OPPOSITE PAGE]** A granary, or food-storage structure, beside Pipe Creek near Indian Gardens, built by the Anasazi Indians about 1,000 years ago.
PHOTO BY TOM BEAN

Grand Canyon lies in "Indian Country." Paleo-Indians, the first humans to see the Canyon, arrived there at least 11,000 years ago. Several Indian cultures used the area for varying periods of time. Today, three Indian tribes—Havasupai, Hualapai, and Navajo—are in the Canyon region.

## SPLIT-TWIG ANIMAL FIGURINES

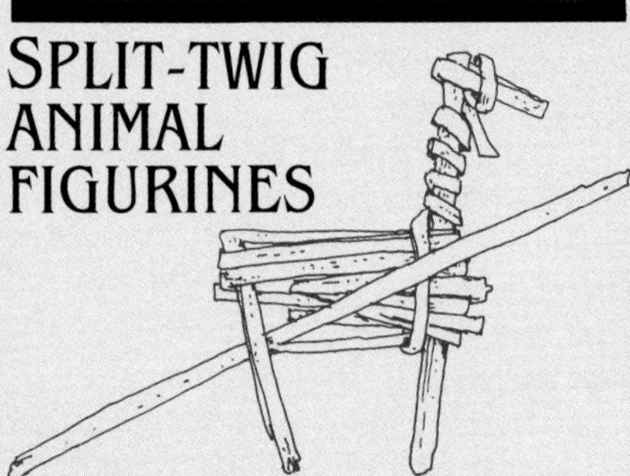

Split-twig animal figurines are the earliest evidence of humans at the Grand Canyon. Made by Archaic Indians, some of the figurines are believed to be about 4,000 years old. A hunting and gathering people, the Archaic may have used the animal figurines as fetishes to invoke magical powers for successful hunts. Some of the figurines are pierced by small twigs, probably representing spears.

**Steps followed by Archaic Indians in making split-twig animal figurines**

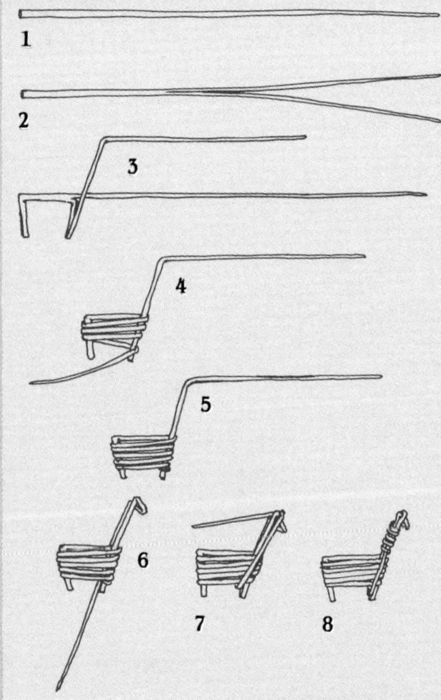


Split-twig animal figurines were crafted by Archaic Indians from single green willow twigs, which were partially split, then twisted into animal shapes.

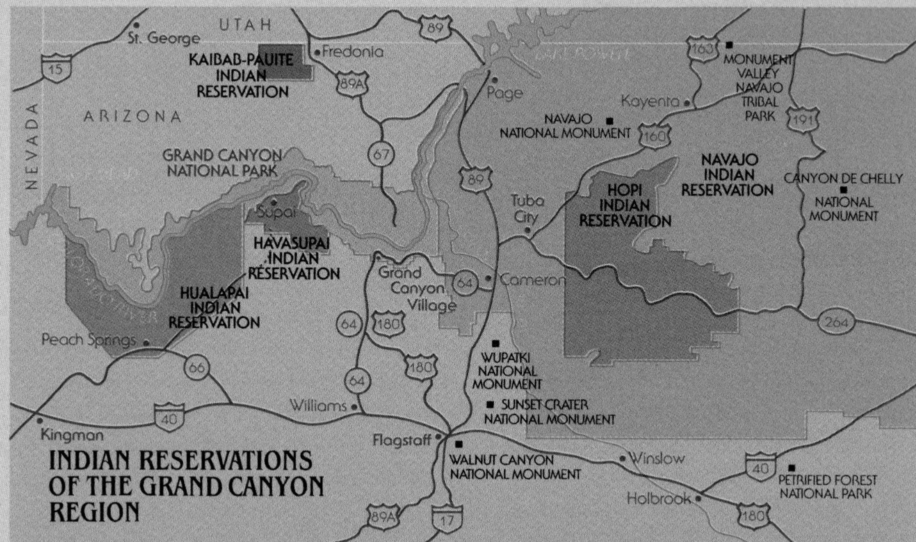

A Havasupai woman and child beside a brush wickiup, photographed in the late 1800s. Havasupai Indians live in the western Grand Canyon region. Their reservation includes Havasu Canyon, which extends south from the Colorado River. In Havasu Canyon is Supai, the Indians' small, isolated village. No roads run to Supai, but it is accessible by trails. Havasu Canyon is noted for several dramatic waterfalls.

PHOTO FROM U.S. DEPARTMENT OF THE INTERIOR, GRAND CANYON NATIONAL PARK, IDENTIFICATION NUMBER 5117

# TUSAYAN PUEBLO

Tusayan Pueblo, an Anasazi Indian village, was constructed in about A.D. 1185. Artist John D. Dawson has depicted the probable appearance of the intact structures. Ruins of the pueblo lie next to East Rim Drive, some three miles west of Desert View, on the Grand Canyon's South Rim. The Anasazi, ancestors of today's Hopi Indians, inhabited the Grand Canyon from approximately A.D. 500 to 1200. More than 2,000 Anasazi sites have been found at the Canyon.

Examples of Anasazi Indian artifacts found at the Grand Canyon.

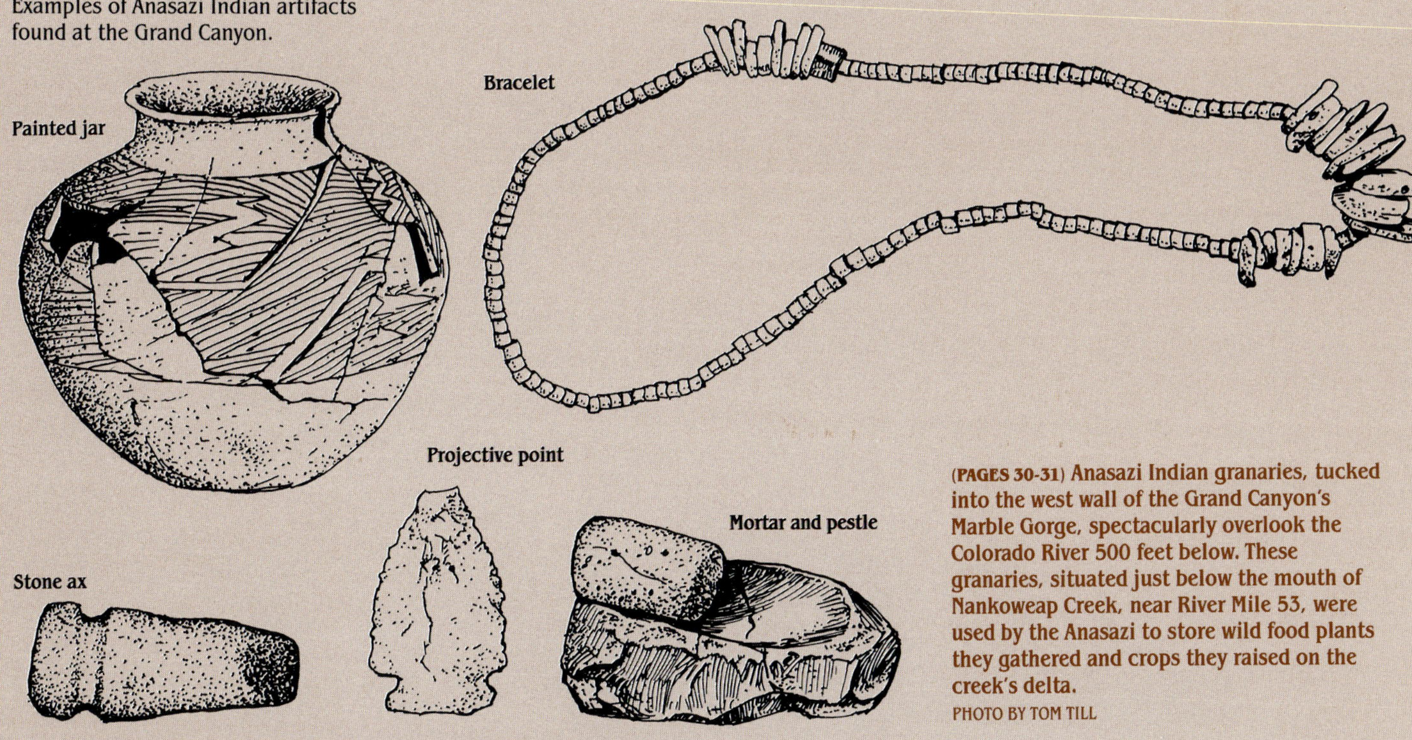


**(PAGES 30-31)** Anasazi Indian granaries, tucked into the west wall of the Grand Canyon's Marble Gorge, spectacularly overlook the Colorado River 500 feet below. These granaries, situated just below the mouth of Nankoweap Creek, near River Mile 53, were used by the Anasazi to store wild food plants they gathered and crops they raised on the creek's delta.

PHOTO BY TOM TILL

Perched on the brink of the Grand Canyon at Yavapai Point, famed artist Thomas Moran sketches the striking panorama before him. Moran's landscape paintings and illustrations of the Canyon did much to bring its grandeur to the public's attention and to achieve national park status for the impressive chasm. Moran, born in England in 1837, emigrated to the United States when he was seven years old. He first saw the Grand Canyon while serving as artist on explorer John Wesley Powell's expedition to the North Rim in 1873. Although not on either of Powell's two Colorado River runs in the Canyon, Moran furnished illustrations for Powell's now historic report, *The Exploration of the Colorado River of the West*, published in 1875. One of Moran's Canyon landscapes, *The Chasm of the Colorado*, an oil painted in 1873-74, measuring seven by twelve feet, was purchased by the U.S. Congress for the Capitol building where it hung until 1950. Then, the enormous canvas was moved to the Museum of the Department of the Interior. Moran returned many times to the Grand Canyon, using it as the subject for paintings. He died in 1926, at the age of 89. Moran Point, on the South Rim, commemorates the great artist.

PHOTO FROM U.S. DEPARTMENT OF THE INTERIOR, GRAND CANYON NATIONAL PARK, IDENTIFICATION NUMBER 5120

# HISTORY

One of the illustrations Thomas Moran provided for John Wesley Powell's accounts of his Grand Canyon explorations depicts the scene at the mouth of the Little Colorado. In this view, Moran has captured both the monumentality and the dramatic beauty of the Canyon. Since the artist was not on either Powell's 1869 or 1872 boat expedition in the Canyon, Moran had to create his drawing from a photo taken on August 23, 1872 by an expedition photographer.

Celebrated worldwide as a marvel of nature, the Grand Canyon is often used as a standard against which other features are measured. Unquestionably spectacular, the Canyon is most often recognized for its size, beauty, and geologic significance. But the Canyon's human history—how people have reacted to the great chasm and how they have used or ignored it—is also a significant and fascinating part of the Grand Canyon's story.

People have come from throughout the world to the Canyon. Travel industry rankings of the ten principal tourist attractions in the United States have consistently included the Grand Canyon, often at the top of the list.

In earlier times, however, the chasm's ruggedness, vastness, and intangible qualities were not so widely appreciated. When, in 1540, the Grand Canyon was discovered by whites—a detachment of the fortune-hunting Coronado Expedition—they saw the chasm only as an enormous obstacle, blocking their way. Other early travelers saw the Canyon as "horrid," and as a "profitless locality."

With the rise of Romanticism—a literary and artistic movement originating in Europe during the eighteenth century—people developed an appreciation for natural landscapes. But even though the Grand Canyon is today highly regarded for its scenic grandeur, there are still those who do not find enjoyment there, among them one who emphatically stated that he "would not give fifteen cents" for the whole area. Another observer who tersely expressed the negative view was The Reverend C. B. Spencer, who, in about 1900, wrote of the Grand Canyon: "Horror! Tragedy! Silence! Death! Chaos! There is the awful canyon in five words."

But for most people, the words of author John L. Stoddard aptly express their sentiments: "To stand upon the edge of this stupendous gorge, as it receives its earliest greeting from the god of day, is to enjoy in a moment compensation for long years of ordinary uneventful life."

## Joseph Christmas Ives

Religious persecution of Mormons in Illinois eventually resulted in the first United States government exploring expedition to the Grand Canyon. In 1847, the Mormons fled to Utah, then part of Mexico. The year before, the United States had declared war on Mexico. America won, and on February 2, 1848 the Treaty of Guadalupe Hidalgo was signed, in which Mexico ceded its northern territory to the victor. This vast area now comprises much of the western United States—including the Grand Canyon. Ten years after the Mexican War, friction developed between the United States government and the Mormons. Convinced that they were in a state of rebellion, President James Buchanan ordered army troops to Utah in 1857 to ensure federal authority. The army believed that a southern supply route to troops in Utah might be needed, but little was known about the region's geography. So, Army Lieutenant Joseph Christmas Ives, of the Corps of Topographical Engineers, led an expedition to find the head of steamboat navigation on the lower Colorado, and to explore the southern Colorado Plateau.

After surveying the River by boat, the Ives expedition traveled eastward to the plateau. Reaching Peach Springs Canyon, in what is now northern Arizona, the party descended the ever-deepening canyon to its junction with Diamond Creek, then followed the creek north to the Colorado, arriving at the bottom of the Grand Canyon on April 2, 1858. There, Dr. John Strong Newberry made the first geological examinations of the chasm. Havasu Canyon was also entered by some of the party. From the Grand Canyon, the expedition trekked to its destination, Fort Defiance, in eastern Arizona. The Mormon unrest was soon resolved, eliminating any need for a southern supply route to the army in Utah. Ives, in his report, concluded that the Grand Canyon was "valueless"—a highly inaccurate observation.

DRAWING BY JOHN D. DAWSON

# SIGNIFICANT EVENTS IN THE GRAND CANYON'S HUMAN HISTORY

Grand Canyon's prehistory began with the arrival of Paleo-Indians, about 11,000 years ago. The historic period was initiated when Spaniards discovered the Canyon in 1540.

DRAWING BY JOHN D. DAWSON

**1540** García López de Cárdenas, with a detachment from the Coronado Expedition, discovered the Grand Canyon. The Coronado Expedition had trekked north from Mexico in search of the fabled riches of the Seven Cities of Cíbola. Where the Cárdenas party reached the Canyon's rim is not known. The locale was probably on the South Rim, perhaps between Desert View and Moran Point.

**1776** Francisco Tomás Garcés, a Franciscan missionary, descended into what is now called Havasu Canyon. From there Garcés traveled east and at the South Rim named what is today the Grand Canyon "Puerto de Bucareli," or Bucareli Pass, a pass for the Colorado, in honor of the Viceroy of New Spain, Antonio María de Bucareli y Ursúa.

The Domínguez-Escalante Expedition, seeking a route from New Mexico to California, reached the Colorado near the head of the Grand Canyon, at the site of what would later become Lee's Ferry.

**1821** Mexico gained independence from Spain. Grand Canyon passed to Mexican control.

**1826** American fur trappers, including James Ohio Pattie, may have seen the Grand Canyon

**1828** George C. Yount led a fur-trapping party which is reported to have reached the bottom of the western Grand Canyon by descending Spencer Canyon to the Colorado.

**1848** Treaty of Guadalupe Hidalgo ended the Mexican War. United States won from Mexico most of what is now the American West, including the Grand Canyon.

**1857-58** Army Lieutenant Joseph Christmas Ives led the first United States government exploring expedition to the Grand Canyon. Dr. John Strong Newberry made the first geological studies of the Canyon.

Dr. John S. Newberry
PHOTO FROM U.S. DEPARTMENT OF THE INTERIOR, GRAND CANYON NATIONAL PARK, IDENTIFICATION NUMBER 3332

**1864** Octavius Decatur Gass, James Ferry, a man named Butterfield, and an unidentified Indian are the first prospectors known to have entered the Grand Canyon. They also made the first recorded boat trip by whites in the chasm, pulling up the Colorado 19 miles into the western Grand Canyon.

**1866** William H. Hardy prospected in Havasu Canyon.

**1867** James White claimed to have rafted completely through the Grand Canyon.

James White
PHOTO FROM HENRY E. HUNTINGTON LIBRARY

**1868** The name Grand Canyon first appeared on a map.

**1869** John Wesley Powell, a one-armed Union Army veteran of the Civil War, led the first documented boat run through the Grand Canyon.

**1871** John Doyle Lee, a Mormon, established a ferry on the Colorado near the mouth of the Paria River, at the head of the Grand Canyon.

**1871** Army Lieutenant George Montague Wheeler led an oar-powered boat expedition up the Colorado into the western Grand Canyon to Diamond Creek.

**1871-72** Second Powell Expedition descended the Colorado River, ending at the mouth of Kanab Canyon, about 51 percent of the way through the Grand Canyon.

John D. Lee
PHOTO FROM ARIZONA HISTORICAL SOCIETY

George M. Wheeler
DRAWING FROM U.S. GEOLOGICAL SURVEY

## POWELL'S RIVER EXPEDITIONS

In 1869, John Wesley Powell led the first documented expedition to travel completely through the Grand Canyon by boat. This river run is one of the great epics in the exploration of Western America. Essentially a private venture, the 1869 expedition had only limited aid from the federal government and from other sources. At the start, the party consisted of nine men, and four boats. Embarking on May 24 from the town of Green River, Wyoming, Powell's party descended the Green River to the Colorado. On this part, one boat was destroyed and one man quit. Then they continued downriver through Cataract Canyon, Glen Canyon—now holding Lake Powell—and finally the Grand Canyon. At what is now Separation Rapid, three more men—concluding it was unsafe to go on—abandoned the voyage. They disappeared and probably were killed by Shivwits Indians, a band of Paiutes that live north of the Canyon. Powell ended the expedition below the Canyon, at the mouth of the Virgin River. The expedition had taken ninety-eight days and covered 1,048 miles. In 1872, Powell led a second River expedition, sponsored by the federal government, about half way through the Canyon, leaving the River at the mouth of Kanab Canyon.

John Wesley Powell, in December 1869, after he returned to Illinois from his first River expedition through the Grand Canyon.
PHOTO FROM UTAH STATE HISTORICAL SOCIETY

Boats of Powell's second expedition, on August 21, 1872 in Marble Gorge, near River Mile 34.5.
PHOTO FROM U.S. GEOLOGICAL SURVEY

**1873** Charles Spencer discovered silver in Havasu Canyon.

**1875** Powell's official report *The Exploration of the Colorado River of the West*, with 29 illustrations by famed artist Thomas Moran, was published by the Government Printing Office.

**1876** Harrison Pearce established a ferry just beyond the western end of the Grand Canyon. His name is often misspelled "Pierce."

**1879** W.C. Beckman and H.J. Young, with other prospectors, found lead in Havasu Canyon.

**1880** James Mooney, a prospector, fell to his death in Havasu Canyon, near the falls which later were named for him.

**1880-81** Clarence Edward Dutton led the first major geological expedition in the Grand Canyon region. He wrote the first monograph on the Canyon's geology, which contained illustrations by Thomas Moran and William Henry Holmes. An atlas accompanied the monograph.

**1882** Senator Benjamin Harrison of Indiana introduced a bill to create the Grand Canyon as a national park. His effort was unsuccessful.

**1883** Senator Harrison again tried, and failed, to establish a national park at the Grand Canyon.

**1883** John Hance became the first white resident of the Grand Canyon. Date of his arrival is uncertain but was probably 1883.

**1884** Emma Burbank Ayer may have been the first white woman to have descended into the depths of the Grand Canyon.

Farlee Hotel, the Grand Canyon's first tourist facility, opened. Located in the western Canyon, the structure was near the chasm's bottom, at the junction of Peach Springs Canyon and Diamond Creek, about 1 mile from the Colorado. The hotel, in 1885, was described as "a board shanty of a single room below, with a kitchen attached, and two bedrooms under the roof above."

William Wallace Bass established a camp on the South Rim, near Havasupai Point, about 27 miles west of the present Grand Canyon Village.

**1885** Bass began offering tourist accommodations at his camp.

**1886** John Hance advertised tourist accommodations at his ranch on the South Rim, near Grandview Point, and guide services.

Senator Harrison made another effort, and failed to establish a national park at the Grand Canyon.

**1889** Farlee Hotel ceased operations.

Farlee Hotel
PHOTO FROM MOHAVE COUNTY HISTORICAL SOCIETY

# The Canyon and The River: How They Got Their Names

## THE RIVER OF MANY NAMES

The Colorado has had many names. Indians living along the River called it by different titles. The Pimas called it the Buqui Aquimuri, the Yumas termed it HahWeal, the Havasupai knew it as the Hakatai, the Paiute name was Pa-ha-weap, the Navajos called it Pocket-to, and the Hopi referred to it as Pi-sish-bai-yu. In 1539, Francisco de Ulloa, a Spaniard, commanding three ships, discovered the River's mouth at the head of the Gulf of California. Ulloa, however, did not name his discovery. The following year, Hernando de Alarcón also sailed to the mouth, and gave the River its first name: "El Río de Buena Guía," or The River of Good Guidance. Also in 1540, Melchior Díaz traveled overland to the River, which he named "Río del Tisón," or the Firebrand River, after the burning sticks carried by local Indians to warm themselves. In 1604, Juan de Oñate, Spanish governor of the province of New Mexico, journeyed to the Colorado. He called it "Río de Buena Esperanza," or River of Good Hope. By the late 1600s, the Colorado was known by its present title, although who precisely named it is a mystery. In 1701, Eusebio Francisco Kino, a Jesuit priest and explorer, prepared a map on which the River is labeled "Río Colorado del Norte." *Colorado* is Spanish for "reddish," probably a reference to the River's often brownish-red color. The name has evolved to its Anglicized form, Colorado River.

Late afternoon shadows darken the Colorado River. Vista from South Rim near Desert View, looking north.
PHOTO BY TOM TILL

## BY ANY OTHER NAME, IT'S STILL GRAND

In 1540, when García López Cárdenas and his expedition discovered the Grand Canyon, they did not give it a name. More than two centuries were to pass before—in 1776—the Canyon was given its first title by whites. Then Franciscan missionary Francisco Tomás Garcés named it "Puerto de Bucareli," or Bucareli Pass, because the chasm formed a pass for the Colorado. Garcés chose the title to honor Antonio María de Bucareli y Ursúa, the viceroy of New Spain. Following the Mexican War, the United States gained possession of most of what is today the American Southwest, including the Grand Canyon. By the 1850s, the chasm was being called "Big Cañon," and "Grand Cañon of the Colorado," names drawn from both Spanish and English. *Cañon* is the Spanish spelling of *Canyon*. "Grand Canyon" eventually became the standard form.

**Robert Brewster Stanton**
PHOTO FROM U.S. DEPARTMENT OF THE INTERIOR, GRAND CANYON NATIONAL PARK, IDENTIFICATION NUMBER 5578

**1889-90** Survey party in boats ran a line along the Colorado River for the proposed Denver, Colorado Canyon, and Pacific Railroad. In 1889, three members of the party drowned in Marble Gorge. Robert Brewster Stanton, the chief engineer, completed the survey. This was the second expedition to descend the Colorado through the Canyon.

**1890** Ben Beamer, a prospector, built a cabin at the mouth of the Little Colorado.

Peter D. Berry located the "Last Chance" copper claim on Horseshoe Mesa below Grandview Point.

**1890-91** Bright Angel Trail built by a group of prospectors. The route followed an old Havasupai Indian path.

**1891** Louis D. Boucher, "The Hermit," a French-Canadian, arrived at the Canyon. He was a prospector, who built tourist facilities at Dripping Springs, and offered his guide services.

**1893** Daniel Hogan located the "Lost Orphan Mine" below Maricopa Point.

President Benjamin Harrison proclaimed the Grand Canyon Forest Preserve.

**1894** William Wallace Bass married Ada Diefendorf, a tourist from New York. She became the first white woman to live at the Canyon. They raised the first white family at the Canyon.

**1895** J. Wilbur Thurber purchased Hance's hotel.

**Grand View Hotel**
PHOTO FROM U.S. DEPARTMENT OF THE INTERIOR, GRAND CANYON NATIONAL PARK, IDENTIFICATION NUMBER 4885

John Hance became the first postmaster at the Grand Canyon. The post office was called Tourist, Arizona.

The Grand View Hotel opened for business on the South Rim at Grandview Point.

**1902** Oliver Lippincott drove the first automobile to the Grand Canyon, a steam-powered Toledo Eight.

**1902-05** Francois Emile Matthes, of the U.S. Geological Survey, made the first topographical maps of the Canyon.

**Ellsworth and Emery Kolb**
PHOTO FROM KOLB COLLECTION, SPECIAL COLLECTIONS LIBRARY, NORTHERN ARIZONA UNIVERSITY, IDENTIFICATION NUMBER 568-16-2-3A

**George Wharton James**
PHOTO FROM SOUTHWEST MUSEUM

**Bright Angel Hotel**
PHOTO FROM U.S. DEPARTMENT OF THE INTERIOR, GRAND CANYON NATIONAL PARK, IDENTIFICATION NUMBER 4499

**1896** Thurber started the Bright Angel Hotel at Grand Canyon Village.

George F. Flavell and Ramon Montos became the third party to boat the length of the Grand Canyon.

**1897** Nathaniel T. Galloway and William C. Richmond, fur trappers, ran the Colorado through the Grand Canyon, the fourth party to complete the run.

**Louis D. "The Hermit" Boucher**
PHOTO FROM U.S. DEPARTMENT OF THE INTERIOR, GRAND CANYON NATIONAL PARK, IDENTIFICATION NUMBER 5972

**John George Verkamp**
PHOTO FROM U.S. DEPARTMENT OF THE INTERIOR, GRAND CANYON NATIONAL PARK, IDENTIFICATION NUMBER 5254

John George Verkamp, an early curio dealer at the Grand Canyon, had his first store in a tent.

**1900** George Wharton James's guidebook, *In and Around the Grand Canyon*, was published.

**1901** First scheduled passenger train arrived at Grand Canyon Village.

Martin Buggeln acquired the Bright Angel Hotel from J. Wilbur Thurber.

**First car at Canyon, 1902.**
PHOTO FROM U.S. DEPARTMENT OF THE INTERIOR, GRAND CANYON NATIONAL PARK, IDENTIFICATION NUMBER 5122

**First passenger train to Grand Canyon, 1901.**
PHOTO FROM U.S. DEPARTMENT OF THE INTERIOR, GRAND CANYON NATIONAL PARK, IDENTIFICATION NUMBER 2435

**1903** Emery and Ellsworth Kolb established a photography studio at Grand Canyon Village.

Cameron Hotel in operation on the South Rim at Grand Canyon Village. Ralph H. Cameron, the hotel's owner, was later a United States senator from Arizona.

**Cameron Hotel**
PHOTO FROM KOLB COLLECTION, SPECIAL COLLECTIONS LIBRARY, NORTHERN ARIZONA UNIVERSITY, IDENTIFICATION NUMBER 568-3-23-1B

Elias "Hum" Woolley, Arthur Sanger, and John King completed the fifth known River transit of the Grand Canyon.

President Theodore Roosevelt visited the Grand Canyon, and said about the chasm in a speech there: "Keep this great wonder of nature as it now is . . . Leave it as it is. You cannot improve on it; not a bit. The ages have been at work on it, and man can only mar it. What you can do is to keep

**Kolb Studio, and Bright Angel Toll Road.**
PHOTO FROM KOLB COLLECTION, SPECIAL COLLECTIONS LIBRARY, NORTHERN ARIZONA UNIVERSITY, IDENTIFICATION NUMBER 568-772

it for your children, your children's children and for all who come after you, as one of the great sights which every American, if he can travel at all, should see. Keep the Grand Cañon as it is."

**"Uncle Jim" Owens**
PHOTO FROM KOLB COLLECTION, SPECIAL COLLECTIONS LIBRARY, NORTHERN ARIZONA UNIVERSITY, IDENTIFICATION NUMBER 568-14-52-1B

**Rust's Camp**
PHOTO FROM U.S. DEPARTMENT OF THE INTERIOR, GRAND CANYON NATIONAL PARK, IDENTIFICATION NUMBER 5434

**1903-24** Ralph Cameron controlled the Bright Angel Trail, and charged a toll to travelers.

**1904-05** El Tovar Hotel built by the Fred Harvey company.

**1906** Martin Buggeln sold the Bright Angel Hotel to the Fred Harvey company.

Grand Canyon Game Reserve was set aside. James T. "Uncle Jim" Owens was appointed warden, and lived on the North Rim.

**1906-18** Owens claimed to have killed 532 mountain lions. On his cabin was a sign reading: "Lions Caught to Order, Reasonable Rates."

**1907** E.D. Woolley, with his son-in-law, David D. Rust, and others installed a cable car across the Colorado near the mouth of Bright Angel Creek.

Rust's Camp, the forerunner of today's Phantom Ranch, established.

**El Tovar Hotel**
PHOTO FROM U.S. DEPARTMENT OF THE INTERIOR, GRAND CANYON NATIONAL PARK, IDENTIFICATION NUMBER 3678

**1908** President Theodore Roosevelt proclaimed Grand Canyon National Monument.

Charles S. Russell and Edwin R. Monett, prospectors, made the sixth water transit through the Grand Canyon.

**1909** First cars reached the North Rim, a Locomobile and a Thomas Flyer.

A party of boaters, organized by wealthy industrialist Julius Stone and guided by Nathaniel T. Galloway, made the seventh trip through the Canyon.

**1910-12** West Rim Drive constructed.

**1911** Sharlot M. Hall, writer, poet, historian, and first woman to hold public office in Arizona, visited North Rim.

**Sharlot M. Hall**
PHOTO FROM SHARLOT HALL MUSEUM, IDENTIFICATION NUMBER PO-160PB

## THE WIT AND WISDOM OF JOHN HANCE

**John Hance at the bottom of the Grand Canyon, standing beside the Colorado River, spinning one of his tales.**
PHOTO FROM U.S. DEPARTMENT OF THE INTERIOR, GRAND CANYON NATIONAL PARK, IDENTIFICATION NUMBER 6263

*To see the Canyon only, and not to see Captain John Hance, is to miss half the show.*

CHESTER P. DORLAND

John Hance was the first white settler on Grand Canyon's South Rim. Although the exact year of his arrival is not known, it was about 1883. A colorful personality, Hance established the first tourist accommodations on the South Rim, at a site east of Grandview Point. His background is veiled by the mists of history—and by his own reticence. Born in Tennessee about 1845, he may have served in the Confederate Army during the Civil War. He was called "Captain," but where this title came from is not known. At the Canyon he was involved in many activities, including mining. After selling his tourist camp in 1895, he became a guide for the Fred Harvey company. Hance died in 1919, and is buried in the Grand Canyon Village cemetery. Hance became a legend for his tall tales about the Canyon. Representative of his many humorous stories are:

- Asked how he lost the tip of one finger, Hance replied that he had worn it off pointing at the Grand Canyon.
- Once, said Hance, he tried to jump his horse across the Canyon. But instead, horse and rider started falling to the bottom. So, Hance claimed, he just halted his horse about three feet above the Canyon floor and stepped off—unhurt.
- When the Canyon was full of fog, Hance related, he would put on snowshoes and walk across to the North Rim. But one time the fog began to dissipate, and he had to land on the summit of Zoroaster Temple. There he was marooned for several weeks until another heavy fog filled the Canyon.

Buckey O'Neill, an early Grand Canyon prospector, once said: "God made the Canyon, John Hance the trails. Without the other, neither would be complete."

William Wallace Bass established the first school at the Canyon.

Bill introduced in Congress to make the Grand Canyon "Carnegie National Park."

**1911-12** Ellsworth and Emery Kolb made the eighth River run through the Canyon, in two boats.

**1912** Arizona became the 48th state.

**1913** After former president Theodore Roosevelt stayed at Rust's Camp, its name was changed to Roosevelt's Camp.

**1914** Hermit's Rest constructed. It was designed by Mary Elizabeth Jane Colter, architect for the Fred Harvey company from 1902 to 1948.

Mary Elizabeth Jane Colter
PHOTO FROM MARY COLTER LARKIN SMITH

Ellsworth Kolb's book, *Through the Grand Canyon from Wyoming to Mexico*, an account of the boat run he and his brother, Emery, made is 1911-12, published.

**1916** National Park Service established.

First airplane to land in the Canyon, 1922.
PHOTO FROM U.S. DEPARTMENT OF THE INTERIOR, GRAND CANYON NATIONAL PARK, IDENTIFICATION NUMBER 5255

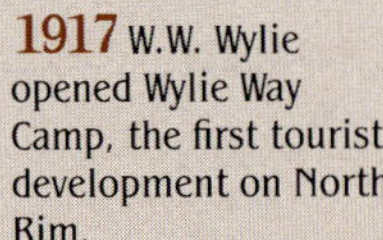

**1917** W.W. Wylie opened Wylie Way Camp, the first tourist development on North Rim.

United States Senator Henry Fountain Ashurst, of Arizona, and United States Representative Carl Hayden, of Arizona, introduced bills to establish the Grand Canyon as a national park.

**1919** Grand Canyon became a national park.

Automobiles allowed on West Rim Drive.

Three DeHaviland Liberty army planes made the first flights over the Canyon.

John Hance died, buried in the cemetery at Grand Canyon Village.

**1920** Fred Harvey company became the principal park concessionaire on the South Rim.

**1921** The first Kaibab Suspension Bridge, a swinging span, placed across the Colorado near mouth of Bright Angel Creek.

Babbitt Brothers Trading Company opened store at Grand Canyon Village.

**1922** Phantom Ranch, designed by Colter, built.

R.V. Thomas landed an airplane on Plateau Point, below Grand Canyon Village on the Tonto Platform.

**1923** Colonel Claude H. Birdseye led the U.S. Geological Survey River expedition through the Canyon. This was the ninth successful run of the Canyon.

**1926-32** Paved roads completed to Point Imperial and Cape Royal on North Rim.

**1927** Clyde Eddy led the tenth boating expedition through the Canyon.

**1928** Swinging Kaibab Suspension Bridge replaced with a rigid span.

Grand Canyon Lodge completed near Bright Angel Point, on North Rim.

Three colorful members of the U.S. Geological Survey Colorado River expedition, 1923.
PHOTO FROM THE U.S. GEOLOGICAL SURVEY

Glen and Bessie Hyde
PHOTO FROM KOLB COLLECTION, SPECIAL COLLECTIONS LIBRARY, NORTHERN ARIZONA UNIVERSITY, IDENTIFICATION NUMBER 568-4-17-12D

First Kaibab Suspension Bridge
PHOTO FROM U.S. DEPARTMENT OF THE INTERIOR, GRAND CANYON NATIONAL PARK, IDENTIFICATION NUMBER 5118

Glen and Bessie Hyde, on their honeymoon, attempted to run the Colorado. Their scow was found, undamaged, a few miles downriver from Diamond Creek, in the western Canyon. The Hydes, however, were never found.

**1929** Park Naturalist Glen Sturdevant and Ranger Fred Johnson drowned attempting to cross the Colorado in a boat above Horn Creek Rapid.

Navajo Bridge opened. It spans Marble Gorge and the Colorado, 4.5 miles downriver from Lee's Ferry.

**1931** Ferde Grofé wrote his muscial composition *Grand Canyon Suite*.

**1932** Watchtower at Desert View constructed. Mary Elizabeth Jane Colter was its architect.

Grand Canyon Lodge on North Rim destroyed by fire.

## FRED HARVEY

*Fred Harvey? Do you know the name? If not, then your education has been much neglected.*

ELBERT HUBBARD'S EULOGY

The name "Fred Harvey"is seen so often at the South Rim that it appears to be almost a synonym for the "Grand Canyon." Though the name is well known to Park visitors, the Fred Harvey it stands for is actually a business—the principal authorized concessionaire of the South Rim, since 1920. However, few people today know who the man behind the name really was. Born in England in 1835, Frederick Henry Harvey emigrated to the United States at age fifteen. In 1876, at Topeka, Kansas, Harvey opened his first restaurant. When he died in 1901, Harvey's enterprises included restaurants, hotels, newsstands, and dining cars on the Santa Fe Railroad. His role in making America's "Wild West" more comfortable won him the title "Civilizer of the West."

PHOTO FROM FRED HARVEY, INC.

**William Wallace Bass**

PHOTO FROM U.S. DEPARTMENT OF THE INTERIOR, GRAND CANYON NATIONAL PARK, IDENTIFICATION NUMBER 3635

**1937** Haldane "Buzz" Holmstrom completed the first accredited solo run of the Colorado through the Grand Canyon.

The California Institute of Technology-Carnegie Institution expedition made a River run through the Canyon. The purpose was to conduct geological investigations.

**1941** Alexander "Zee" Grant ran the first kayak through the Canyon.

**1942** Otis R. "Dock" Marston, who later became a Colorado River historian and boatman, made his first trip through the Canyon, as a passenger with Nevills.

**Grand Canyon, Lodge, 1930.**

PHOTO FROM U.S. DEPARTMENT OF THE INTERIOR, GRAND CANYON NATIONAL PARK, IDENTIFICATION NUMBER 8157

**Grand Canyon Lodge destroyed by fire, 1932.**

PHOTO FROM U.S. DEPARTMENT OF THE INTERIOR, GRAND CANYON NATIONAL PARK, IDENTIFICATION NUMBER 577

**1933** William Wallace Bass died. He was cremated and his ashes were dropped on Holy Grail Temple, which is now also known as Bass Tomb.

**1934** "Dusty Dozen" River expedition, so called because of the low-water stage, made the eleventh run through the Canyon.

**1935** Bright Angel Lodge opened.

**1936** Reconstruction of Grand Canyon Lodge began.

**1938** Amos Burg ran the first rubber raft through the Canyon.

Norman Nevills began commercial river-running in the Canyon. On this run were two women botanists from the University of Michigan, Elzada Urseba Clover and Lois Jotter. They studied plants along the River.

**1944** Harry Aleson organized an expedition to attempt an upriver run in the Grand Canyon with an outboard motorboat. The boat, *Up Lake*, reached River Mile 221, where it hit a rock, wrecking the motor.

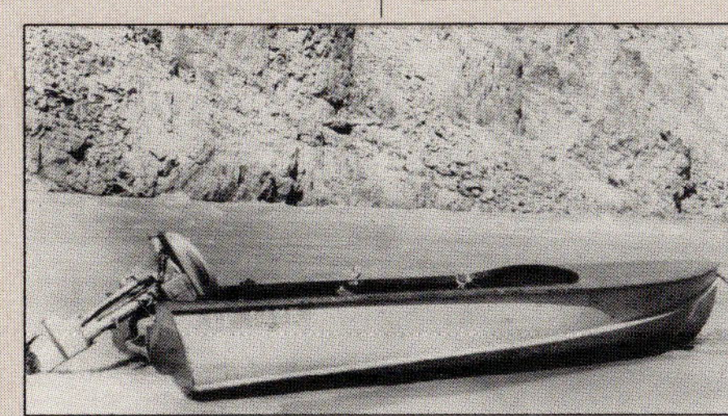

**Harry Aleson's motorboat, *Up Lake*.**

PHOTO FROM UTAH STATE HISTORICAL SOCIETY

**Bert Loper**

PHOTO FROM ARIZONA HISTORICAL SOCIETY

**1948** Ed Hudson attempted an upriver run, in the *Esmeralda II*. The crew included "Dock" Marston. The boat did not have enough power to get through 217-Mile Rapid.

**1949** Including Powell's 1869 crew, 100 different people had boated completely through the Canyon.

Bert Loper capsized in 24½-Mile Rapid and died, probably of a heart attack.

Hudson ran the first motorboat, the *Esmeralda II*, downriver from Lee's Ferry through the Canyon. Included in the crew was "Dock" Marston.

**1954** First commercial use of inflated rafts by Bus Hatch.

**Norman Nevills, at Bright Angel Creek, 1947.**

PHOTO FROM U.S. DEPARTMENT OF THE INTERIOR, GRAND CANYON NATIONAL PARK, IDENTIFICATION NUMBER 1584

**Alexander "Zee" Grant, ran first kayak through Canyon, 1941. Photo by Weldon Heald.**

PHOTO FROM U.S. DEPARTMENT OF THE INTERIOR, GRAND CANYON NATIONAL PARK, IDENTIFICATION NUMBER 5012

**1955** William K. Beer and John Daggett swam from Lee's Ferry to Pearce Ferry.

**1956** P.T. Reilly discovered and named Keyhole Bridge, a large natural opening through Redwall Limestone, in the western Grand Canyon.

Two airliners on eastward flights collided over the Canyon and crashed near the mouth of the Little Colorado, killing all 128 people aboard the two planes.

**1959** William G. Cooper organized an up-Canyon run with 2 boats powered by outboard motors, but they could not surmount Lava Falls.

**1960** Bob Smith attempted an up-Canyon run in a boat powered by 2 outboard motors, but was stopped by Lava Falls.

First successful up-Canyon run used Buehler Turbocrafts powered by marine motors, fitted with jet propulsion units. "Dock" Marston was one of the crew. One of the boats, *Wee Yellow*, sank in Grapevine Rapid.

**1974** Pioneer river-runner and Canyon photographer Emery C. Kolb, 93 years old, flown by helicopter to the junction of the Colorado and Little Colorado. There Kolb boarded a Grand Canyon Expeditions raft for a two-day run to below Crystal Rapid, where he was lifted out of the Canyon by helicopter.

**1976** Emery Kolb died, at age 95, and was buried at Grand Canyon Village cemetery. His death marked the end of the pioneering era at the Grand Canyon.

# SOUTH RIM

At the Grand Canyon, the Abert squirrel occurs only on the South Rim. This tree squirrel closely resembles the Kaibab squirrel, whose total range is restricted to the North Rim. Both squirrels are tassel-eared, and are of the same size and gray color, except that the Abert's belly is white while the Kaibab's is gray, and the Abert's tail is gray on top with a white underside while the Kaibab's is all white.
DRAWING BY JOHN D. DAWSON

**[OPPOSITE PAGE]** Canyon vista from Yaki Point, on the East Rim Drive. The viewpoint, at an altitude of 7,260 feet, was named for the Yaqui Indians of Mexico.
PHOTO BY TOM TILL

**[PAGES 40-41]** February snow blankets the Grand Canyon, extending down to the chasm's bottom and coating Phantom Ranch near mouth of Bright Angel Canyon. View from the South Rim.
PHOTO BY GARY LADD

NEARLY ALL OF THE CANYON'S tourist facilities are on the South Rim. Open year round, the South Rim is the most visited area of the Park, with Grand Canyon Village the focus of visitor activities.

Additional accommodations and services are in Tusayan, a small town located on Arizona Highway 64 about eight miles south of the Village and two miles from the Park's entrance station. Adjacent to Tusayan is Grand Canyon Airport.

Panoramatic vistas of the Canyon can be viewed from many points along the South Rim. Two roads run along or near the Canyon's edge: East Rim Drive, and West Rim Drive.

■ East Rim Drive branches from the south entrance road, about one-and-a-half miles north of the Park's entrance station and three miles southeast from Grand Canyon Village. This drive runs twenty-one miles to Desert View and the Park's east entrance station. Tourist services at Desert View are limited, but include a general store, souvenir shop, a gasoline station, and a campground. Tusayan Ruins, an Anasazi Indian pueblo built about A.D. 1185, lies three miles west of Desert View. Next to the ruins is a museum. East Rim Drive provides access to the head of South Kaibab Trail, which begins near the tip of Yaki Point. South Kaibab Trail connects at the Colorado River with North Kaibab Trail, which heads on the North Rim, to form a hiking route which runs twenty-one miles across the Canyon. Yaki Point is one mile east of the East Rim Drive's junction with the south entrance road.

■ West Rim Drive begins at the western edge of Grand Canyon Village, near the head of Bright Angel Trail. This scenic road parallels much of the Canyon's edge for eight miles to Hermit's Rest, where there is a souvenir shop.

Altitudes on the South Rim range from 6,000 to 7,500 feet, or about 1,000 to 1,500 feet lower than the North Rim's. Grand Canyon Village is 6,860 feet above sea level. Elevations along East Rim Drive are higher than those along West Rim Drive.

Average annual precipitation for the South Rim is 14.46 inches, and mean yearly snowfall measures 64.9 inches. January is the coldest month, with an average temperature of 30.5°F. A record low of −16°F. was set in 1949. July is the warmest month, with a mean of 69.4°F. The highest temperature observed was 98°F. in June 1933.

The South Rim is part of the Coconino Plateau. Its surface is formed by Kaibab Limestone, a yellow-gray rock. Many types of fossil invertebrates (animals without backbones) have been found in this formation.

Two major vegetative communities are on the South Rim: the piñon-juniper woodland, found in the West Rim Drive area, and the yellow-pine woodland, common along the East Rim Drive. The piñon-juniper woodland is generally at elevations lower than the yellow-pine woodland. Piñon pines and junipers are short evergreens, usually twenty feet or less in height, that form open woodlands. Yellow pines, also called ponderosa, are much taller, with mature trees reaching heights of 125 feet.

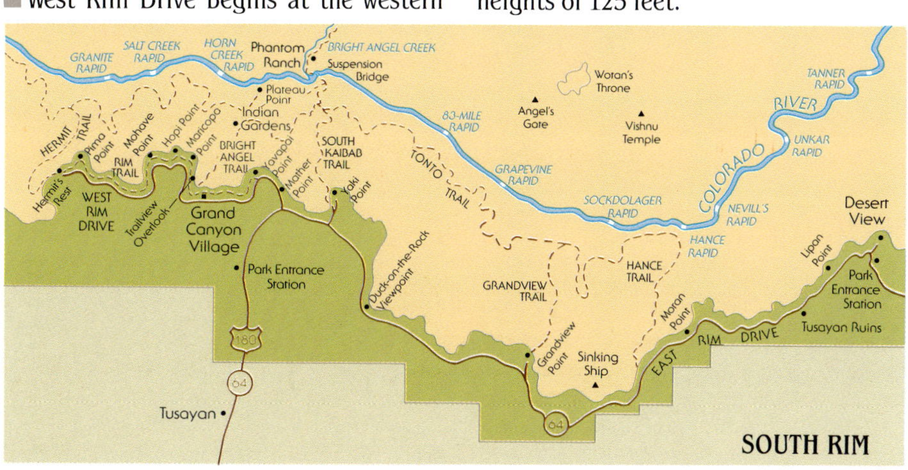

[OPPOSITE PAGE] From the South Rim's Mather Point, much of Bright Angel Canyon is visible. Bright Angel Creek cut its canyon along the Bright Angel Fault in a nearly straight line for more than eleven miles.
PHOTO BY FRANK L. MENDONCA

[TOP] Duck-on-the-Rock, a fancifully named pillar of Kaibab Limestone, stands beside East Rim Drive on the Canyon's brink.
PHOTO BY TOM TILL

[BOTTOM] Sunrise colors from Mather Point, with Isis Temple rising in mid-Canyon.
PHOTO BY TOM TILL

**[OPPOSITE PAGE]** A departing winter storm leaves snowfall on Mather Point. The Canyon overlook was named in honor of Stephen Tyng Mather (1867-1930), the first director of the National Park Service.
PHOTO BY TOM TILL

**[BELOW]** Early morning colors and shadows in the Canyon, from Hopi Point on the West Rim Drive. The overlook, at an altitude of 7,071 feet, was named for the Hopi Indians of Arizona.
PHOTO BY JERRY SIEVE

**[TOP]** Canyon panorama from Moran Point on the East Rim Drive. The vantage point, at an elevation of 7,138 feet, was named for English-born artist Thomas Moran (1837-1926), whose landscaping paintings, including those of the Grand Canyon, brought him fame in America, his adopted home.
PHOTO BY TOM TILL

**[BOTTOM]** Banana yucca at the rim's edge, along the West Rim Drive.
PHOTO BY TOM TILL

**[OPPOSITE PAGE]** From Mohave Point on the West Rim Drive, the Colorado River—more than three-quarters of a mile below—reflects storm light. The point, at an altitude of 6,974 feet, was named for the Mohave Indians, whose reservation lies along the Colorado downstream from the Grand Canyon.
PHOTO BY TOM TILL

**[PAGES 50-51]** From Mather Point, the Canyon's buttes and ridges are silhouetted against rays of early morning sunlight beneath a bank of heavy clouds.
PHOTO BY DICK DIETRICH

# NORTH RIM

**Bobcats range throughout the Grand Canyon, including the North Rim.**
DRAWING BY JOHN D. DAWSON

HEAVY SNOWFALL—in an average winter almost 130 inches are recorded—coupled with the area's remoteness, limits the North Rim's tourist season to the summer. This district of the Park generally closes after the first snowfall, usually in October, and normally reopens in May.

The North Rim's isolation is strikingly apparent at night, when lights on the South Rim—less than 11 airline miles across the Canyon are prominently visible from Grand Canyon Lodge. Yet by road, the distance from the Lodge to the South Rim's Village is nearly 214 miles!

North Rim visitor accommodations and services are limited, and include a general store, a gasoline filling station, and a campground. Grand Canyon Lodge, near the tip of Bright Angel Point, offers the only lodgings on the North Rim. The lodge has a restaurant and a souvenir shop. Additional tourist facilities are available five miles north of the Park's entrance station, and at Jacob Lake, thirty-two miles from the entrance and forty-four miles from the lodge. Jacob Lake is located at the junction of U.S. Highway 89A and Arizona Highway 67.

The North Rim is part of the Kaibab Plateau. The Rim's wall is penetrated by large canyons which extend far into the plateau, unlike the South Rim's wall, into which fewer canyons have been eroded.

On the North Rim are the highest altitudes found at the Grand Canyon—up to 9,165 feet, or about 1,500 feet higher than the South Rim.

The North Rim is the Park's coolest and wettest area. Winters are cold, and summers are cool. January, the coldest month, has a mean temperature of 28.7° F. The record low was measured in February 1957 when the thermometer read −25° F. July is the Rim's warmest month, with a mean of 61.7° F. The highest temperature recorded was 91° F. in July 1939.

Mean annual precipitation is 22.78 inches, and the yearly average snowfall is 128.7 inches, or nearly 11 feet.

At the higher North Rim elevations, above 8,200 feet, the cool and moist environment supports a dense spruce-fir forest, interspersed with meadows. A yellow-pine woodland extends from the spruce-fir forest down to an altitude of 7,200 feet. Below the yellow-pine woodland's altitude and along the edges of the rim is a piñon-juniper woodland.

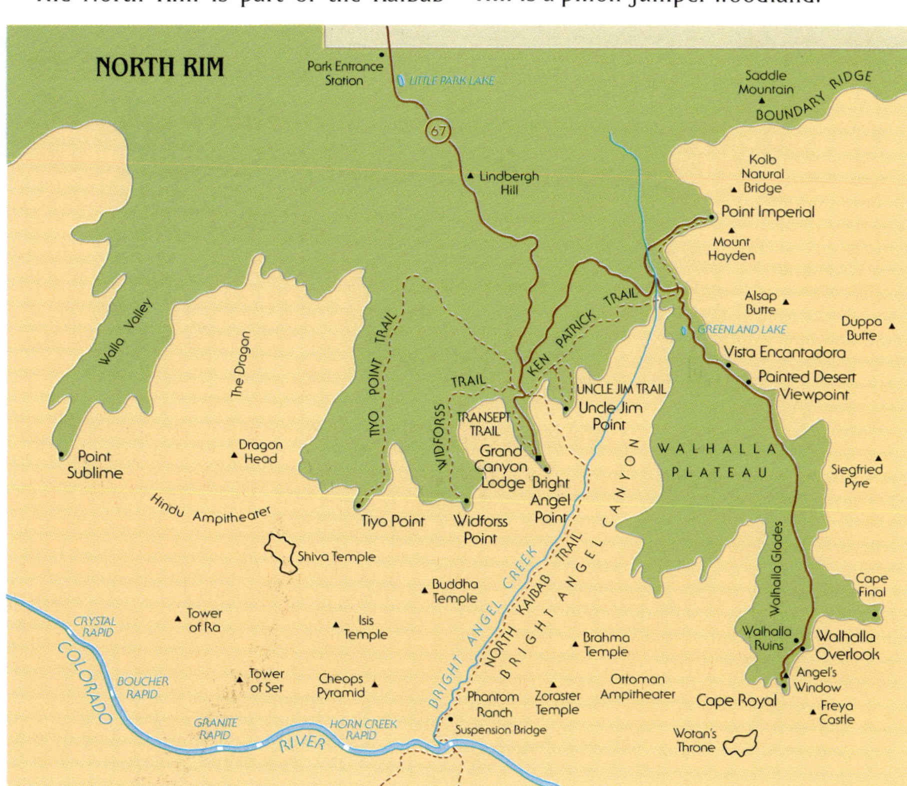


**[OPPOSITE PAGE] Storm clouds darken the Canyon west of the North Rim's Cape Royal.**
PHOTO BY FRANK L. MENDONCA

**[OPPOSITE PAGE]** Angel's Window, a large natural arch near Cape Royal on the North Rim, dramatically frames the Colorado River a mile below.
PHOTO BY TOM TILL

**[TOP]** Aspens aflame with fall colors along the North Rim's Ken Patrick Trail. Winding through the forest along the rim for twelve miles, the route runs from the head of the North Kaibab Trail to Point Imperial. The trail was named in memory of Park Ranger Ken Patrick, who had been assigned to the Grand Canyon's North Rim for several seasons. Patrick was slain in the line of duty at Point Reyes National Seashore, California in 1973.
PHOTO BY FRANK L. MENDONCA

**[BOTTOM]** Aspens reflect on the placid surface of Greenland Lake, a shallow pond on the North Rim.
PHOTO BY TOM TILL

[BELOW] Mount Hayden, a huge, prominent spire, dominates the foreground view from Point Imperial, an overlook at 8,803 feet altitude on the North Rim. Formed by the hard Coconino Sandstone, Mount Hayden projects above the softer, red Hermit Shale. The spire was named in honor of Charles Trumbull Hayden (1825-1900), an Arizona pioneer who founded what is now the city of Tempe.
PHOTO BY TOM TILL

[OPPOSITE PAGE] The Colorado River flows 3,000 feet below Toroweap Overlook, a vantage point on the edge of the Esplanade in the western Grand Canyon.
PHOTO BY GARY LADD

[PAGES 58-59] Flat-topped Wotan's Throne from Cape Royal on the North Rim, with the Canyon's broad, level South Rim stretching east to west on the horizon.
PHOTO BY DICK DIETRICH

# BENCHLANDS

Bighorn sheep are found in the Grand Canyon on the Benchlands and along the Colorado River and its tributaries.
DRAWING BY JOHN D. DAWSON

LYING BELOW THE CANYON RIMS and above the inner gorges of the Colorado River are two broad terraces which collectively constitute the Benchlands: the Tonto Platform, and the Esplanade.

**Tonto Platform**

One of the most prominent topographical features of the central Grand Canyon is the Tonto Platform. It lies about 3,000 feet below the Canyon's rims and some 1,000 to 1,500 feet above both sides of the Colorado River. The terrace's general altitude is 3,000 to 4,000 feet. In some places its width extends to three miles. The Tonto Platform begins in Marble Gorge, just above the junction of the Little Colorado River with the Colorado. In the western Grand Canyon, the Tonto Platform is not as well developed as it is in the central Canyon.

Floored by erosion-resistant Tapeats Sandstone, the Tonto Platform developed when the weaker, overlying Bright Angel Shale was eroded from the harder sandstone. The Bright Angel Shale is a greenish-gray, fine-grained, and generally thin-bedded formation. It is approximately 400 feet thick, and is of Cambrian age, or some 600 million years old. The Tapeats Sandstone is brownish, conspicuously bedded, and coarse textured. The unit is 100 to 300 feet thick and forms a distinctive cliff immediately below the Tonto Platform.

The Tonto has a semi-arid climate. Desert-scrub plants characterize the vegetation of the terrace. These drought-resistant plants are low, woody-stemmed, and spaced far apart. The Tonto's dominant plant is the blackbrush. A small, densely branched, spiny shrub with short, narrow, dark-green leaves, it grows in shallow soils that are sandy, often somewhat rocky, and low in salinity.

**Esplanade**

One of the major landforms of the western Canyon is a hummocky terrace called the Esplanade. In places it is some five miles wide. It lies at higher elevations than the Tonto Platform. Altitudes for the Esplanade are generally 4,000 to 5,000 feet. Toroweap Overlook, on the Esplanade's edge and about 3,000 feet above the Colorado River's north bank, is at an elevation of 4,552 feet.

The Esplanade developed as the weak Hermit Shale was stripped away from the more resistant Supai Sandstone. The thin-bedded, maroon Hermit Shale varies in thickness from between 200 to more than 1,000 feet. It is of Permian age, forming some 280 million years ago. The Supai Sandstone is a thick-bedded, red formation. It is 600 to 700 feet thick, and was deposited during the Pennsylvanian and Permian, or 310 to 230 million years ago.

The Esplanade's climate is semi-arid. At the Tuweep Ranger Station, near Toroweap Overlook, yearly precipitation averages 11.38 inches.

Vegetation is sparse, and includes various desert-scrub species and representatives of the piñon-juniper woodland.

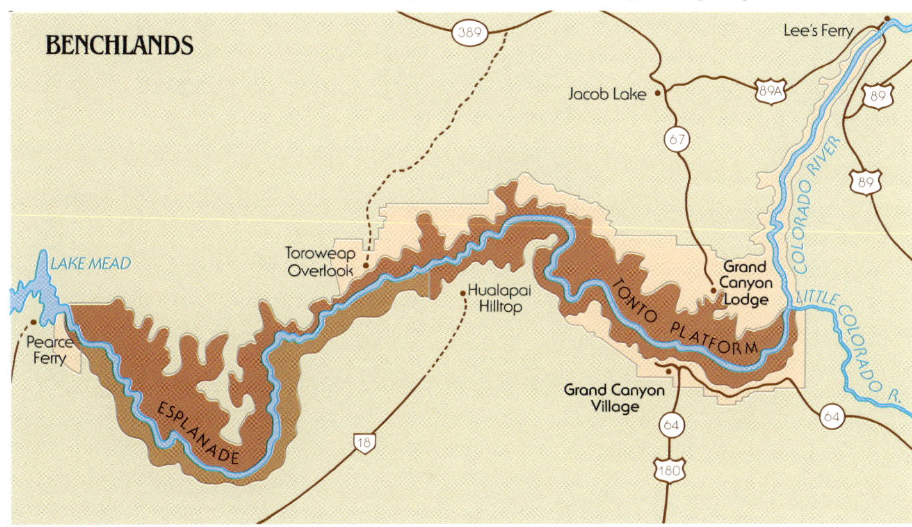


[OPPOSITE PAGE] Morning in late April on the Tonto Platform, at the foot of Hall Butte.
PHOTO BY GARY LADD

[PAGES 62–63] Rainwater-filled potholes near Toroweap Overlook on the Esplanade create temporary pools on the rocky surface. The prominent gash across the hummocky terrace marks the deep inner gorge of the Colorado River.
PHOTO BY TOM TILL

# HAVASU CANYON

Fremont Cottonwoods are found within the Grand Canyon along tributaries to the Colorado, both permanent streams—such as Havasu Creek—and seasonal watercourses. But the trees are rare on the banks of the Colorado River.

DRAWING BY JOHN D. DAWSON

IN THE WESTERN GRAND CANYON, south of the Colorado River, Havasu Canyon—which has also been called Cataract Canyon—cuts far into the Coconino Plateau. Havasu, one of the major side gorges of the Grand Canyon, joins the Colorado at River Mile 156.7. Most of northern Havasu Canyon is in the Havasupai Indian Reservation. The reservation covers about 300 square miles, plus nearly 150 square miles of Grand Canyon National Park land between the reservation and the Colorado, which has been set aside as a traditional-use area for the Indians.

Deep within Havasu Canyon lies Supai, the small, isolated village of the Havasupai Indians. The tribe's name means "the people who live at the place which is green," an apt description of their oasis-like canyon home surrounded by arid, rocky terrain.

Nearly half a mile below Havasu Canyon's rim, Supai is not easily accessible to the outside world. The closest road ends about eight miles from the Indian village. This road, Indian Route 18, begins at Arizona State Highway 66, seven miles east of Peach Springs, and runs northeast sixty-one miles—much of it across the Hualapai Indian Reservation—to Supai's trailhead at Hualapai Hilltop. The trail drops to the bottom of Hualapai Canyon, runs down the gorge to its junction with Havasu Canyon, then goes downstream along Havasu Creek to Supai. From Supai, the trail continues down canyon, passing Havasu Canyon's waterfalls, to the Colorado River, nine miles north from Supai.

The blue-green waters of Havasu Creek rise at Havasu Spring, about a mile up the canyon from Supai. Along its entrenched course to the Colorado, Havasu Creek generates four dramatic waterfalls. The three closest to the Indian village are the largest.

Navajo Falls, one-and-a-half miles downstream from the Indian village, hurtles some seventy-five feet. It was probably named for Chief Navajo, a Havasupai leader who died in 1898.

A half mile beyond Navajo Falls the creek makes a spectacular lunge of nearly 100 feet at Havasu Falls. It has also been called "Bridal Veil Falls," a name derived from an earlier time when its lip was much wider, giving the falling water a veil-like appearance.

Another mile north, or three miles below Supai, Mooney Falls plummets 196 feet—the greatest drop of the canyon's waterfalls. This fall was named for James Mooney, a prospector who fell to his death near the site in 1880.

Beaver Falls, with a drop of some thirty feet, is the fourth and smallest of the significant drops on Havasu Creek. Named for the semiaquatic mammals that live along the creek, Beaver Falls lies two miles below Mooney Falls, or five miles from Supai, and four miles up Havasu Creek from the Colorado. Beaver Cascades, a series of rapids and several large pools, are nearby.

Havasu Canyon's climate is more moderate than the climate on either the South Rim or the North Rim. Supai, at an altitude of 3,195 feet above sea level, lies nearly three-quarters of a mile lower than Grand Canyon Village on the South Rim, and more than a mile lower than Point Imperial on the North Rim.

At Supai, January's average temperature is 40.1°F. The record low was −4°F. in December 1961. July has a mean temperature of 83.2°F. The highest temperature measured was 111°F. in July 1971. Average yearly precipitation is only 8.36 inches. Normal annual snowfall amounts to a scant 2.1 inches.

HAVASU CANYON
KANAB CREEK
CANYON
COLORADO RIVER
DEER CREEK
GRAND
FISHTAIL RAPID
DUBENDORFF RAPID
UPSET RAPID
HAVASU RAPID
BEDROCK RAPID
BEAVER FALLS
MOONEY FALLS
HAVASU FALLS
NAVAJO FALLS
NATIONAL
HAVASU CREEK
Supai
Havasu Spring
LEE CANYON
HAVASUPAI
PARK
BEAVER CANYON
HUALAPAI CANYON
TRAIL
Hualapai Hilltop
INDIAN
RESERVATION
CANYON

[OPPOSITE PAGE] Havasu Falls, one of the most exquisite waterfalls in the world, has a plunge of nearly 100 feet. Below the falls, Havasu Creek cascades over small, crescent-shaped dams formed by travertine deposits.

PHOTO BY DAVID MUENCH

[OPPOSITE PAGE] Deeply entrenched Havasu Canyon has four major waterfalls, with Mooney Falls and Havasu Falls the most significant. Mooney, the highest, plunges 196 feet from a horseshoe-shaped cliff, and Havasu—a mile up Havasu Creek from Mooney—drops nearly 100 feet.
PHOTO BY P.T. REILLY

[BELOW] Cascades on Havasu Creek.
PHOTO BY DIANNE DIETRICH LEIS

[PAGES 68-69] Mooney Falls was named for James Mooney, a prospector who fell to his death near the falls in 1880.
PHOTO BY DAVID MUENCH

# COLORADO RIVER

Beaver live in the Grand Canyon along the Colorado River and its perennial tributaries, such as Bright Angel Creek.
DRAWING BY JOHN D. DAWSON

**[OPPOSITE PAGE]** Early morning comes to Marble Gorge. Originally named "Marble Canyon" by explorer John Wesley Powell, the title is a misnomer, since there is no marble in the gorge. However, the gorge's prominent Redwall Limestone formation has a polished marble-like appearance in many places, suggesting the name to Powell.
PHOTO BY TOM TILL

THE COLORADO RIVER FLOWS through the entire length of the Grand Canyon—277.7 miles. Distances along the River are measured downstream from Lee's Ferry at the Canyon's head, which has been designated Mile 0.

The Colorado drops some 1,900 feet through the Canyon, from Lee's Ferry at 3,116 feet above sea level, to the fluctuating level of Lake Mead, which backs into the Canyon some forty miles. The River's average drop is 8.1 feet per mile, but the gradient is much steeper in rapids.

Although rapids constitute only nine percent of the River's length, fifty percent of its drop occurs in them. There are 161 recognized rapids, but the actual number at any given time depends upon the water flow. Rapids form where rock debris has been deposited, usually at the mouths of tributary streams. More rapids form at low-water stages than at high, when the flow is less blocked. Rapids average 1.6 miles apart.

Prior to 1963, when Glen Canyon Dam began to control the Colorado's discharge through the Grand Canyon, the River's recorded flows varied from less than 1,000 cubic feet per second (c.f.s.) to 325,000.

The amount of sediment transported by the River through the Canyon also has been affected by the dam. Before its construction, the total averaged about 143 million tons per year, although the load was much greater in some years. In 1927, 480 million tons were recorded.

The Colorado's width in the Canyon is generally between 200 and 300 feet. Its narrowest spot—about 60 feet—occurs in mile-long Granite Narrows, which begins at Mile 135.1. The River's depth varies, depending upon its discharge. At a flow of 48,500 c.f.s., the depth averages about 50 feet, with its deepest measured point of 110 feet at Mile 114.3.

Average velocity of the River's flow at 48,500 c.f.s. in smooth water is 4.2 miles per hour (m.p.h.), and in rapids generally 7.5 to 10 m.p.h.

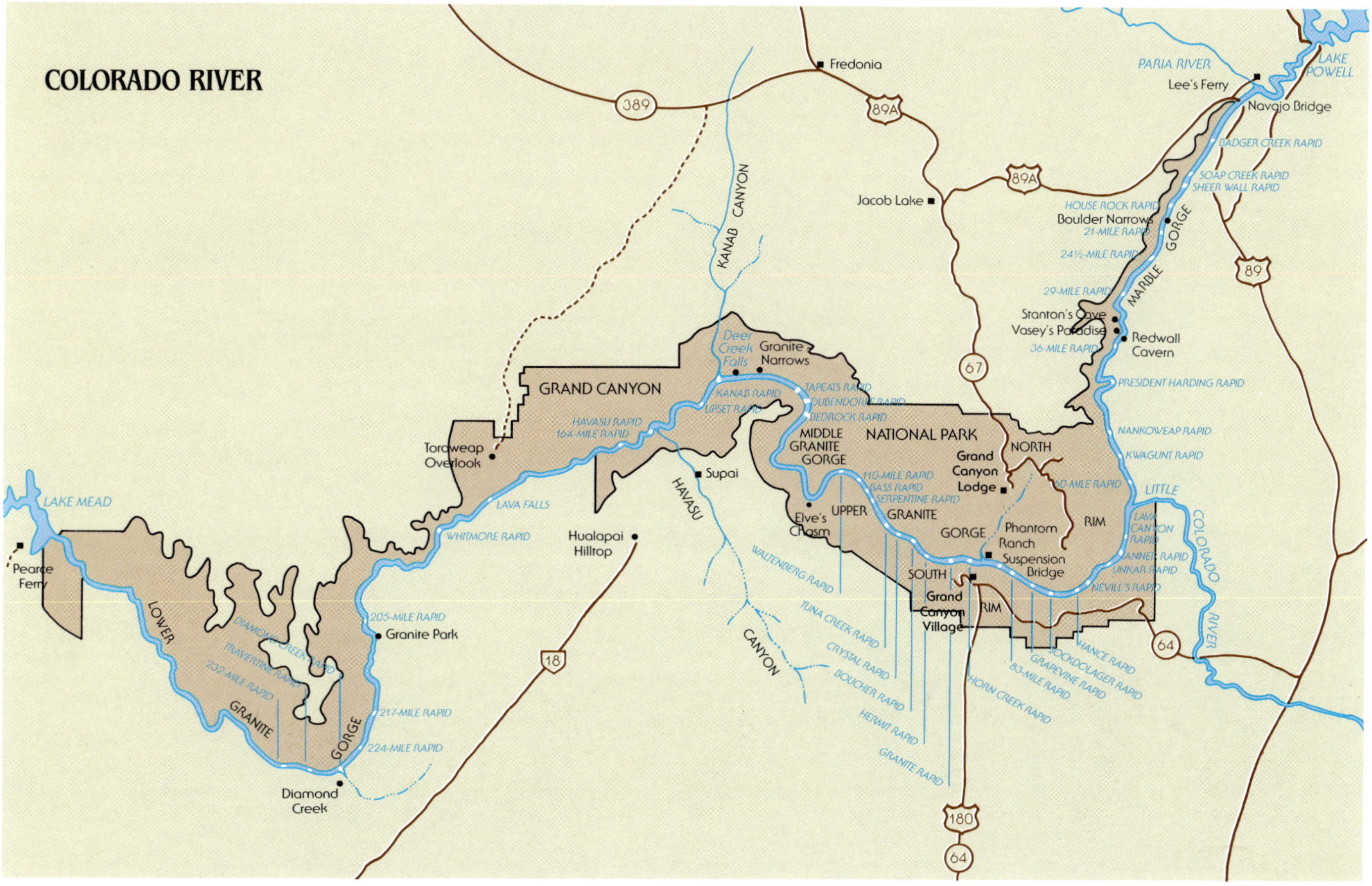

COLORADO RIVER

Fredonia
389
89A
Jacob Lake
PARIA RIVER
Lee's Ferry
LAKE POWELL
Navajo Bridge
BADGER CREEK RAPID
SOAP CREEK RAPID
SHEER WALL RAPID
HOUSE ROCK RAPID
Boulder Narrows
21-MILE RAPID
24½-MILE RAPID
MARBLE GORGE
89
29-MILE RAPID
Stanton's Cave
Vasey's Paradise
36-MILE RAPID
Redwall Cavern
PRESIDENT HARDING RAPID
NANKOWEAP RAPID
KWAGUNT RAPID
KANAB CANYON
67
Deer Creek Falls
Granite Narrows
GRAND CANYON
TAPEATS RAPID
DUBENDORFF RAPID
KANAB RAPID
UPSET RAPID
BEDROCK RAPID
HAVASU RAPID
164-MILE RAPID
MIDDLE GRANITE GORGE
NATIONAL PARK
NORTH
Grand Canyon Lodge
RIM
Toroweap Overlook
Supai
HAVASU CANYON
110-MILE RAPID
BASS RAPID
SERPENTINE RAPID
UPPER GRANITE GORGE
Elve's Chasm
LITTLE COLORADO RIVER
LAVA CANYON RAPID
TANNER RAPID
UNKAR RAPID
NEVILL'S RAPID
Phantom Ranch
Suspension Bridge
SOUTH RIM
Grand Canyon Village
LAKE MEAD
LAVA FALLS
WHITMORE RAPID
Hualapai Hilltop
Pearce Ferry
WALTENBERG RAPID
TUNA CREEK RAPID
CRYSTAL RAPID
BOUCHER RAPID
HERMIT RAPID
GRANITE RAPID
HORN CREEK RAPID
83-MILE RAPID
GRAPEVINE RAPID
SOCKDOLAGER RAPID
HANCE RAPID
64
LOWER GRANITE GORGE
DIAMOND CREEK RAPID
TRAVERTINE RAPID
232-MILE RAPID
205-MILE RAPID
Granite Park
217-MILE RAPID
224-MILE RAPID
18
Diamond Creek
180
64

**[OPPOSITE PAGE]** Kwagunt Rapid on the Colorado, at River Mile 56 in Marble Gorge. "Kwagunt" was the name of a Paiute Indian who was friendly to Powell's exploring expedition in 1869.
PHOTO BY TOM TILL

**[TOP]** A Grand Canyon Expeditions neoprene-coated nylon raft, the *Río Virgen*, a thirty-seven foot S-Rig with long side tubes, piloted by Art Gallenson, approaches the head of Hance Rapid at River Mile 76.6.
PHOTO BY TOM TILL

**[BOTTOM]** *Río Virgen* bucks the waves of Lava Falls. In the western Grand Canyon at River Mile 179.3, Lava drops thirty-seven feet. On a scale of 1 to 10 measuring the difficulty of navigating rapids, Lava Falls is ranked 10, the most severe rating.
PHOTO BY TOM TILL

**[OPPOSITE PAGE]** Springs at Vasey's Paradise gush from the Redwall Limestone cliff on the west side of Marble Gorge at River Mile 31.9, creating a verdant tapestry of plants. The springs were named by Powell's 1869 river expedition for George W. Vasey, a botanist on an earlier Powell expedition in the Rocky Mountains.
PHOTO BY TOM TILL

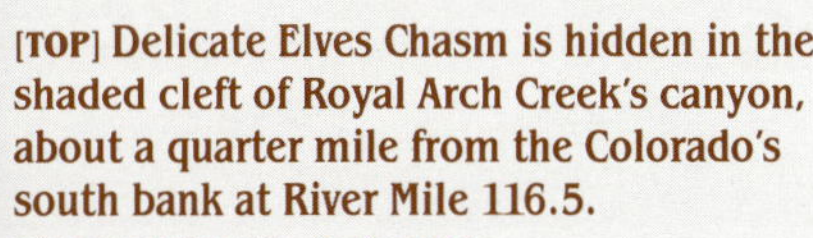

**[TOP]** Delicate Elves Chasm is hidden in the shaded cleft of Royal Arch Creek's canyon, about a quarter mile from the Colorado's south bank at River Mile 116.5.
PHOTO BY FRANK L. MENDONCA

**[BOTTOM]** Deer Creek Falls, on the north side of the Colorado, at River Mile 136.2.
PHOTO BY FRANK L. MENDONCA

[TOP LEFT] The colorful travertine bowl of Pumpkin Spring, on the south side of the Colorado at River Mile 213, is exposed only at low water.
PHOTO BY TOM TILL

[TOP RIGHT] Detail of fluted Vishnu Schist, at River Mile 230 on the north wall of the Lower Granite Gorge. The Precambrian-age Vishnu Schist is at least 1.7 billion years old.
PHOTO BY TOM TILL

[BOTTOM] Early morning in National Canyon, a chasm on the south side of the Colorado in the western Canyon, at River Mile 166.5.
PHOTO BY TOM TILL

[OPPOSITE PAGE] The incredible turquoise water of the Little Colorado River blends with the murky flow of the Colorado, at River Mile 61.4. Entering from the east, the Little Colorado marks the lower, or south, end of Marble Gorge.
PHOTO BY TOM BEAN

**[ABOVE]** Pinkish flowers of beavertail cactus bloom on the south bank of the Colorado at River Mile 190.
PHOTO BY FRANK L. MENDONCA

**[OPPOSITE PAGE]** View upstream in Marble Gorge.
PHOTO BY TOM TILL

**[PAGE 80-INSIDE BACK COVER]** Late afternoon in Marble Gorge.
PHOTO BY TOM TILL

**[OUTSIDE BACK COVER]** Newly fallen snow paints a winter landscape on the South Rim's Mather Point.
PHOTO BY TOM TILL